بِسْمِ اللّٰهِ الرَّحْمٰنِ الرَّحِيْمِ

وَرَتِّلِ الْقُرْاٰنَ تَرْتِيْلاًؕ

Tajweed
for
Young Children

A translation of *Baar Tajweed*

By

Moulana (Qari) Dawood Muhammad Limbada (Umarwadi) رحمه الله

Tajweed for Young Children - A translation of *Baar Tajweed* by
Moulana (Qari) Dawood Muhammad Limbada (Umarwadi) ﷺ

ISBN: 978-1-912301-01-0

Published by:
www.tafseer-raheemi.com
info@tafseer-raheemi.com

For comments and corrections about this book, please email
ahlimbada@gmail.com

Tajweed for Young Children
Table of contents

i

PREFACE BY SHAYKH ABDUR RAHEEM IBN QARI DAWOOD LIMBADA

نَحْمَدُهُ وَنُصَلِّيْ عَلٰى رَسُوْلِهِ الْكَرِيْمِ . اَمَّا بَعْدُ .

Reciting Quran with *tajweed* is extremely important. The great Imam of *tajweed*, Imam Jazari ﷺ has said:

وَالْاَخْذُ بِالتَّجْوِيْدِ حَتْمٌ لَازِمٌ

"Implementing *tajweed* is *hatmun laazim* (necessary)."

In 1966, my late father, Qari Dawood Limbada, may Allah have mercy on him, wrote a concise book on tajweed. He was an Imam in Bodhan, Gujarat, India, and his aim was to make *tajweed* accessible for pupils in madrassas.

It was the first book of its kind in the Gujarati language. The book gained widespread acceptance, and was used throughout Gujarat for over 50 years.

My mother tells me that he would first write a passage, and then cut, edit, improve and correct it until he was happy with it. He would look for the simplest examples and he himself taught it for some time before he was encouraged to publish it by the committee of the madrassa.

For over half a century, it remained available only in the Gujarati language. We began to translate it into English while he was still alive, but unfortunately, it did not reach completion. After he passed away, my brother, Moulana Abdul Hafiz, along with the help of my brother-in-law, Qari Ismail Nanabava, completed the translation from Gujarati into English.

We beseech Allah to grant acceptance to this English version as He did to the Gujarati version.

May Allah ﷻ reward my dear respected father, and elevate his ranks in *jannah*. May Allah make this short treatise a *sadqaae jaariyah* (enduring charity) for him. Ameen.

(Shaykh) Abdul Raheem Limbada
21 Shabaan 1438 AH
18th May 2017

1

THE OPINION OF:
DARUL ULOOM JAMIA HUSAINIA, RANDER'S PRINCIPAL
SHEIKH MUHAMMAD SAEED RANDERI

بِسۡمِ اللّٰهِ الرَّحۡمٰنِ الرَّحِيۡمِ

اَلۡحَمۡدُ لِلّٰهِ وَ كَفٰى وَسَلَامٌ عَلٰى عِبَادِهِ الَّذِيۡنَ اصۡطَفٰى. اَمَّا بَعۡدُ

Moulana Qari Dawood Limbada sahib's book, *Tajweed for Young Children*, contains even the smallest rules on the pronunciation of Arabic letters (مَخَارِج) and the rules of Quran recitation (تَجۡوِيۡد). It has been elegantly written, with examples, using clear and simple language.

The contents of this book will help a student to read the Quran with *tajweed*. In the madrassas of Gujarat, India, the book has proved immensely beneficial to students.

We pray that the Almighty bless the book, accept it, and help popularise it far and wide. Ameen.

The Servant:
Moulana Saeed Randeri
Servant of Jamea Hussainia, Rander
14th April 1970

THE OPINION OF:
DARUL ULOOM FALAHE DAARAIN,
TADKESHWAR'S
TEACHER OF TAJWEED:
QARI MUHAMMAD SAALIH ﴿

بِسْمِ اللهِ الرَّحْمٰنِ الرَّحِيْمِ

This small book, *Tajweed for Young Children*, is the first *tajweed* book written in the Gujarati language. It has given the servants of Allah access to *tajweed* learning, and allowed teachers to teach the rules of *tajweed* to others.

The author, the honourable Qari Moulana Dawood Muhammad Limbada of Umarwada, has expended a tremendous amount of effort in producing a unique piece of work for the children of Gujarat.

I consider this work of his to be a huge service to the people. I pray that the Almighty Allah accept this small book forever, and that it is used in the madrassas to support the correct learning of *tajweed*.

The aforementioned book is hugely beneficial for beginning students of *tajweed*, and really should be used to teach them. Therefore, current primary level madrassas are encouraged to integrate this book into their syllabus.

Sincerely yours and in need of your duas:
Muhammad Salih Jogwari
Tajweed Department
Falaah e Daarain
Tadkeshwar
District Surat
12th May 1970

3

THE OPINION OF MY DEAR RESPECTED TEACHER: HAJI MOULANA QARI MUHAMMAD IBRAHIM JARA ﷫, OF NAROLI

اَلْحَمْدُ لِلّٰهِ رَبِّ الْعٰلَمِيْنَ . وَالصَّلٰوةُ وَالسَّلَامُ عَلٰى رَسُوْلِهِ الْكَرِيْمِ اَمَّا بَعْدُ:

Moulana Qari Dawood Muhammad Limbada sahib of Umarwada has done a tremendous favour upon the Muslims of Gujarat, through his Gujarati book Tajweed for young children. The book is in the field of Tajweed and qiraa'ah and is full of Arabic examples. It required a huge amount of effort and this effort should be celebrated and he should be congratulated.

For this reason, I make an earnest appeal to the Muslims of Gujarat that they benefit from this book and use it to correct their reading of the Quran.

They should introduce this book into the primary syllabus, so that they produce students who read Quran correctly from the very beginning. Thus, they will always be protected from the sin and curse of incorrect recitation and be able to act upon the hadiths of the Prophet ﷺ to gain the reward of both worlds:

Hadith: The Prophet ﷺ has said: "There are many people who recite the Quran, but the Quran curses them (because they recite incorrectly)."

May Allah protect us from the curse of incorrectly reading the Quran. Ameen.

Finally, I pray that Allah accepts the aforementioned book and makes it a means of success and salvation for the author, publisher, and all those who distribute it.

آمِيْنُ يَا رَبَّ الْعٰلَمِيْنَ. فَقَطْ وَالسَّلَام .

The Sinful One - In need of your prayers
Muhammad Ibrahim Jara, former teacher of *tajweed*
Madressa Jamia Husainia, Rander, District Surat
Currently located at: Madressa Talimul Islam
Kafue, Zambia, Africa
8th May 1973

Author's Foreword to the 4th Edition

نَحْمَدُهُ وَنُصَلِّيْ عَلٰى رَسُوْلِهِ الْكَرِيْمِ . اَمَّا بَعْدُ:

The reciting and reading of the Quran is both important and rewarding for the Muslims, but for it to be a real reflection of the words of Allah, it must be recited with *tajweed*, which is a field of study that has a lofty status of its own.

The young Muslims of today need Quranic and religious knowledge. Consequently, this difficult field of *tajweed* was in need of a simple book that would allow this knowledge to sink into the minds of children, without it being a burden on them.

Alhamdulillah, for the past 4 years, at Madrassa Taalimul Islam, Bodhan, a Gujarati booklet has been used and included in the syllabus for the teaching of *tajweed*. An effort was made to instil an understanding of the subject into the minds of the children. Our experience showed that the book was highly effective, and to widen the audience and benefit others, we are now making the booklet available to everyone.

The lessons from the booklet mentioned above were shortened and simplified as much as possible, and the new book was called *Baar Tajweed* (*Tajweed for Young Children*). The book has, so far, been through eight reprints.

Through the grace of Allah, *Tajweed for Young Children* was an outstanding success, and very quickly went through 3 editions. With the help of Allah and the support of the public, this 4th edition is being printed. However much we show gratitude to Allah, and to members of the public who have helped, that gratitude will never be enough. We pray that Allah spreads the benefits of this book far and wide and as fast as the wind.

May Allah reward, both in this world and the next, all those people who helped print and publicise this book, and gave financial, verbal, and written support, and gave us their time. May He reward them according to His status, and may He send His special mercy on all of them. Ameen.

This book also contains some of the rules and correct manners for praying the Quran, although, as the saying goes:محبت تجھ کو آداب محبت سکھائے گی – love itself will teach you the manners of love.

To keep this book short, simple and accessible for children, the most complex rules of *tajweed* have been omitted, and for this I apologise.

Teachers are requested to ensure that:

1. Students recite the letters correctly from the very beginning.
2. Once five *paras* or *juz* have been completed, this book should be formally taught as part of the syllabus over a period of 3-4 years,
3. At the start of every year, revision should be done of all material taught in previous years.
4. All rules that have been taught must be applied to the student's Quran recitation immediately and consistently; only then will students be able to faithfully absorb the rules and understand and fully apply them.

We are all human; everybody makes mistakes. We pray that the Merciful Creator, who has given us the ability to serve his Quran, overlooks any mistakes and makes this book a means of eternal salvation.

وَمَا تَوْفِيْقِيْ اِلَّا بِاللّٰهِ. عَلَيْهِ تَوَكَّلْتُ وَاِلَيْهِ اُنِيْبُ

Dawood Muhammad Limbada (of Umarwada)
Former student of Madrassa Jamea Hussainia, Rander
Servant of Madressa Talimul Islam, Bodhan
Currently living in: Dewsbury, UK.
(1974)

بِسْمِ اللهِ الرَّحْمٰنِ الرَّحِيْمِ

وَرَتِّلِ الْقُرْاٰنَ تَرْتِيْلاًۗ

Tajweed
for
Young Children

Part 1

بِسْمِ اللهِ الرَّحْمٰنِ الرَّحِيْمِ

رَبِّ يَسِّرْ وَلَا تُعَسِّرْ وَتَمِّمْ بِالْخَيْرِ

1.1 - GOOD MANNERS WHEN RECITING آدَابُ

تَعَوُّذْ :   اَعُوْذُ بِاللهِ مِنَ الشَّيْطٰنِ الرَّجِيْمِ

تَسْمِيَّةٌ :   بِسْمِ اللهِ الرَّحْمٰنِ الرَّحِيْمِ

RULES OF TA'AWWUZ AND TASMIYYAH اَلتَّعَوُّذُ وَالتَّسْمِيَةُ

1. Before beginning to recite the Quran, you must pray both *ta'awwuz* and *tasmiyyah*.
2. If you stop and say something that isn't part of the quran, pray *ta'awwuz* first, and then carry on reading.
3. When you finish a surah, pray *tasmiyyah*, and then start the next surah.
4. If you want to read verses from another part of the Quran, pray *tasmiyyah* and then read them.

EXERCISE:

Follow the instructions below. Remember to pray ta'awwuz and tasmiyyah where required.

1. Read the 1st verse.
2. Say your name
3. Carry on reading the next 2 verses.
4. Read the last verse

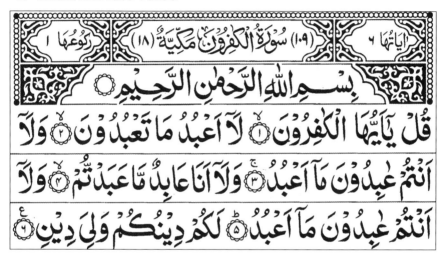

THE RULES FOR SURAH TAWBAH سُوْرَةُ التَّوْبَةِ

The rules for *surah Tawbah* (surah 9) are different.

1. When you reach the end of *surah Anfaal* (surah 8), **do not** pray *tasmiyyah.* Just carry on reading, as if *surah Anfaal* and *surah Tawbah* are one surah.

2. However, if you **start** reading from *surah Tawbah*, then pray both *ta'awwuz* and *tasmiyyah.* This is the opinion of most scholars.

3. **Did you know:** *ta'awwuz* is only prayed when beginning to read the Quran; however, *tasmiyyah* is prayed when beginning any book, including the Quran.

EXERCISE:

Follow the instructions below. Remember to pray ta'awwuz and bismillah where required.

1. Start reading from *surah tawbah* to the end.
2. Read all the lines again, but this time, start from the top of the page.
3. Read the three-line verse only
4. Say your name
5. Carry on reading.
6. Go back and pray the 1st verse of *surah tawbah* again.

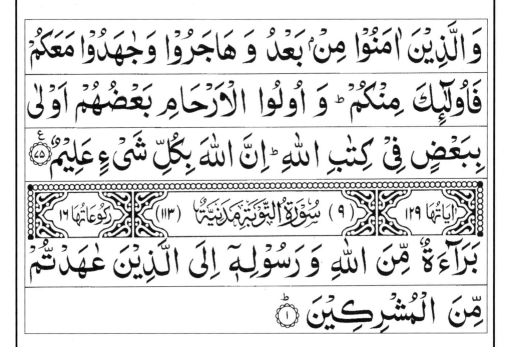

1.2 - MAKHRAJ مَخْرَجُ

WHAT IS TAJWEED تَجُوِيْدُ?

Tajweed (تَجُوِيْد) is a way of reading the Quran in which every letter is spoken from the correct place (*makhraj*) and with the correct characteristics (*sifaat*).

If you don't pray the Quran with *tajweed*, you have committed *Lahn*.

Lahn is reading the Quran incorrectly by not applying the *tajweed* rules. There are 2 types of *lahn*.
1. *Lahn jalii*
2. *Lahn khafii*

LAHN JALII لَحْن جَلِيّ

Lahn jalii are major, obvious mistakes. There are 5 types:

1. Reciting the **wrong letter** in a word eg.

   a. اَلْهَمْدُ ✗

   b. اَلْحَمْدُ ✓

2. Stretching a word by **adding** letters

   a. اِيَّاكا ✗

   b. اِيَّاكَ ✓

3. Shortening a word by **removing** letters

   a. اَنْ طَهَّرَ ✗

   b. اَنْ طَهَّرَا ✓

4. Replacing a *harkat* with a *saakin*

   a. صُحْفًا ✗

   b. صُحُفًا ✓

5. Replacing a *saakin* with a *harkat*

   a. اَنَعَمْتَ ✗

   b. اَنْعَمْتَ ✓

These are all *lahn jalii*, or major mistakes. It is *haram*, or 'completely forbidden', to pray the Quran with *lahn jalii* mistakes.

LAHN KHAFII لَحْن خَفِيّ

Lahn khafii are less obvious mistakes. They are 5 types too:

1. Reciting full mouth letters, like ط غ , with a mouth empty of air.

   غَيْرِالْمَغْضُوْبِ : saying ghayril(✗) instead of ghoyril(✓)

2. Reciting empty mouth letters, like ت, with a mouth full of air.

   الْمُسْتَقِيْمَ : saying mustoqeem (✗) instead of
      a. mustaqeem (✓)

3. Lengthening a letter by praying it with a *madd* (˜)

   قَالَ : saying qaaaaala (✗) instead of qaala (✓)

4. Shortening a letter by praying it without *madd* (˜)

   جَآءَ : saying ja'a (✗) instead of jaaaaaaaa'a (✓)

5. Reading *ikhfa, izhaar* and *ghunnah* the same way, when they should be different

   آمَنَّا : saying Aamannaa (✗) instead of
   Aamannnnnnaa (✓)

13

These are all *lahn khafii*, or less obvious mistakes. It is *makrooh*, or very bad, to recite the Quran with *lahn khafii* mistakes.

PARTS OF THE TONGUE اَللِّسَانْ

In this book, the following parts of the tongue, along with its sides will be referred to. The diagram below shows which area each term refers to.

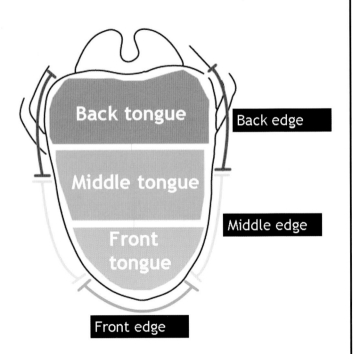

1.3 – مَخَارِج - THE PARTS OF THE TONGUE, MOUTH, TEETH AND THROAT THAT SOUNDS ARE MADE WITH

The *makhraj* of a word tells you which parts of the tongue, mouth, teeth and throat are used to make a sound. Arabic has 29 letters. Their *makhaarij* are given below:

THE MAKHRAJ OF THE HUROOF MADDAH مَدَّة

The letters that are made with an unobstructed rush of air coming out of the mouth are called *huroof maddah*. They are:

ي	و	ا
(يَاء)	(وَاو)	(اَلِفُ)

1. اَلِفُ *maddah* is an *alif*(ا) with a *zabar* (َ) before it eg قَالَ

2. وَاو *maddah* is a *wow saakin* (وْ) with a *pesh* (ُ) before it. eg قُوْلَ

3. يَاء *maddah* is a *yaa saakin* (يْ) with a *zer* (ِ) before it eg قِيْلَ

These 3 letters are called *huroof maddah* and all three are in

the word نُوْحِيْهَا.

Sometimes, they appear as a vertical line above or below a

letter, or as a small number 6 – for example. سُبْحٰنَهٗ and

اَمْرِهٖ.

EXERCISE

Underline all the *huroof maddah* in this verse, and then read it
(there are 16!):

اَلَاۤ اِنَّهُمْ يَثْنُوْنَ صُدُوْرَهُمْ لِيَسْتَخْفُوْا مِنْهُ ۙ اَلَا

حِيْنَ يَسْتَغْشُوْنَ ثِيَابَهُمْ ۙ يَعْلَمُ مَا يُسِرُّوْنَ

وَمَا يُعْلِنُوْنَ ۚ اِنَّهٗ عَلِيْمٌۢ بِذَاتِ الصُّدُوْرِ ۞

Do the same for these verses. There are 25.

اَتٰۤى اَمْرُ اللّٰهِ فَلَا تَسْتَعْجِلُوْهُ ۗ سُبْحٰنَهٗ وَ تَعٰلٰى

عَمَّا يُشْرِكُوْنَ ۞ يُنَزِّلُ الْمَلٰٓئِكَةَ بِالرُّوْحِ مِنْ

اَمْرِهٖ عَلٰى مَنْ يَّشَآءُ مِنْ عِبَادِهٖۤ اَنْ اَنْذِرُوْۤا

اَنَّهٗ لَاۤ اِلٰهَ اِلَّاۤ اَنَا فَاتَّقُوْنِ ۞ خَلَقَ السَّمٰوٰتِ

16

THE MAKHRAJ OF THE HUROOF HALQI حَلْقِيّ

The letters that are taken out from the throat are called *huroof halqi*. They are:

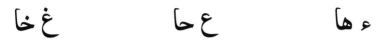

غ خا   ع حا   ء ها

1. ها ء - these come out from the bottom of the throat.

أَءُ   اَهَ

2. ع حا - these come out from the middle of the throat

اَعُ   اَحْ

3. غ خا - these come out from the top of the throat

اَغُ   اَخْ

Note 1: an *alif* with nothing on it is called an *alif*.

قَالَ

Note 2: when an *alif* has a *zabar, zer, pesh* (ˊ ِ ˊ) or *saakin* (ˈ), it is called a *hamza* (ء)

فَأْتِ   اُنْزِلَ   اِنْ اَنْتُمُ

17

EXERCISE

Underline all the huroof halqi in this passage, and then read it:

١. سَخَّرَهَا عَلَيْهِمْ سَبْعَ لَيَالٍ وَّثَمٰنِيَةَ اَيَّامٍ حُسُوْمًا فَتَرَى الْقَوْمَ فِيْهَا صَرْعٰى كَاَنَّهُمْ اَعْجَازُ نَخْلٍ خَاوِيَةٍ

Underline all the huroof halqi in this passage too, and then read it:

٢. جَزَآؤُهُمْ عِنْدَ رَبِّهِمْ جَنّٰتُ عَدْنٍ تَجْرِيْ مِنْ تَحْتِهَا الْاَنْهَارُ خٰلِدِيْنَ فِيْهَآ اَبَدًا رَّضِيَ اللّٰهُ عَنْهُمْ وَرَضُوْا عَنْهُ ذٰلِكَ لِمَنْ خَشِيَ رَبَّهٗ

18

THE MAKHRAJ OF THE HUROOF LAHAWII لَهَوِيّ

A *lahawii* letter is one that is produced by moving the back of the tongue to the *luhaat* (uvula – the soft, fleshy part hanging down at the back of the mouth).

The letters ق and ك are both *lahawii* letters.

1. ق is produced by making the back of the tongue touch the far end of the roof of the mouth

   a. اَقُ

2. ك is produced in a similar way to ق, but the tongue is moved slightly forward, away from the uvula.

   a. اَكُ

EXERCISE

Underline all the huroof lahawii in the verses below, and then read them.

١. اِنَّ هٰذَا كَانَ لَكُمْ جَزَآءً وَّكَانَ سَعْيُكُمْ مَشْكُوْرًا

٢. وَلَقَدْ كَذَّبَ الَّذِيْنَ مِنْ قَبْلِهِمْ فَكَيْفَ كَانَ نَكِيْرٌ

٣. يَآ اَيُّهَا الْاِنْسَانُ اِنَّكَ كَادِحٌ اِلٰى رَبِّكَ كَدْحًا فَمُلَاقِيْهِ

19

4. فَاصْبِرْ لِحُكْمِ رَبِّكَ وَلَا تَكُنْ كَصَاحِبِ الْحُوتِ اِذْ نَادَى وَهُوَ مَكْظُومٌ

5. قُلْ هُوَ الَّذِيٓ اَنْشَاَكُمْ وَجَعَلَ لَكُمُ السَّمْعَ وَالْاَبْصَارَ وَالْاَفْئِدَةَ قَلِيلًا مَّا تَشْكُرُوْنَ

6. قَالُوْا بَلٰى قَدْ جَآءَنَا نَذِيرٌ فَكَذَّبْنَا وَقُلْنَا مَا نَزَّلَ اللهُ مِنْ شَيْءٍ اِنْ اَنْتُمْ اِلَّا فِيْ ضَلَالٍ كَبِيرٍ

7. وَاِنْ يَّكَادُ الَّذِيْنَ كَفَرُوْا لَيُزْلِقُوْنَكَ بِاَبْصَارِهِمْ لَمَّا سَمِعُوا الذِّكْرَ وَيَقُوْلُوْنَ اِنَّهُ لَمَجْنُوْنٌ

8. اِنَّآ اَنْذَرْنٰكُمْ عَذَابًا قَرِيْبًا يَّوْمَ يَنْظُرُ الْمَرْءُ مَا قَدَّمَتْ يَدَاهُ وَيَقُوْلُ الْكَافِرُ يٰلَيْتَنِيْ كُنْتُ تُرَابًا

THE MAKHRAJ OF THE HUROOF SHAJARI شَجَرِيّ

A *shajari* letter is one that is produced by making the middle of the tongue touch the roof of the mouth.

The letters ج , ش, and ياء ***ghayr maddah*** are all *huroof shajari.*

Examples: اَجْ اَشْ اَيْ

Note: ياء ***ghayr maddah*** is any ياء ***saakin*** that **doesn't** have *zer* (ِ)before it, for example, اَيْنَمَا.

EXERCISE

Underline all the huroof shajari in the verses below, and then read them

1. وَجَعَلْنَا سِرَاجًا وَّهَّاجًا

2. وَاصْبِرْ عَلٰى مَا يَقُوْلُوْنَ وَاهْجُرْهُمْ هَجْرًا جَمِيْلًا

3. عَيْنًا يَّشْرَبُ بِهَا عِبَادُ اللهِ يُفَجِّرُوْنَهَا تَفْجِيْرًا

4. وَجَعَلَ الْقَمَرَ فِيْهِنَّ نُوْرًا وَّجَعَلَ الشَّمْسَ سِرَاجًا

٥. يَوْمَ تَرْجُفُ الْأَرْضُ وَالْجِبَالُ وَكَانَتِ الْجِبَالُ كَثِيبًا مَّهِيلًا

٦. اِنَّمَا نُطْعِمُكُمْ لِوَجْهِ اللهِ لَا نُرِيدُ مِنْكُمْ جَزَاءً وَّلَا شُكُورًا

٧. وَاَنَّا لَمَسْنَا السَّمَاءَ فَوَجَدْنَاهَا مُلِئَتْ حَرَسًا شَدِيدًا وَّشُهُبًا

٨. وَيُمْدِدْكُمْ بِاَمْوَالٍ وَّبَنِينَ وَيَجْعَلْ لَّكُمْ جَنَّتٍ وَيَجْعَلْ لَّكُمْ اَنْهَارًا

٩. اِنَّا خَلَقْنَا الْاِنْسَانَ مِنْ نُّطْفَةٍ اَمْشَاجٍ نَبْتَلِيهِ فَجَعَلْنَاهُ سَمِيعًا بَصِيرًا

THE MAKHRAJ OF THE HUROOF HAAFI حَافِي

A *hafii* letter is produced by making the back-right or back-left edge of the tongue lightly touch the edge of the teeth next to it. ض is the only *hafii* letter.

Examples: أَضْ

EXERCISE

Underline all the huroof haafi in the verses below, and then read them.

١. وَكُنَّا نَخُوْضُ مَعَ الْخَآئِضِيْنَ

٢. اِرْجِعِيْ اِلٰى رَبِّكِ رَاضِيَةً مَّرْضِيَّةً

٣. فَاَقْبَلَ بَعْضُهُمْ عَلٰى بَعْضٍ يَّتَلَاوَمُوْنَ

٤. وَقَدْ اَضَلُّوْا كَثِيْرًا وَّلَا تَزِدِ الظَّالِمِيْنَ اِلَّا ضَلٰلًا

٥. صِرَاطَ الَّذِيْنَ اَنْعَمْتَ عَلَيْهِمْ غَيْرِ الْمَغْضُوْبِ عَلَيْهِمْ وَلَا الضَّآلِّيْنَ

THE MAKHRAJ OF THE HUROOF TARAFII طَرَفِيّ

A *tarafii* letter is one that is produced by making the front edges of the tongue touch the area behind the top front teeth.

The letters ل, ن and ر are all *tarafii* letters.

Examples: اَرُ اَنْ اَلُ

EXERCISE

Underline all the huroof tarafii in the verses below, and then read them.

١. اِنَّآ اَرْسَلْنَآ اِلَيْكُمْ رَسُوْلًا شَاهِدًا عَلَيْكُمْ كَمَآ اَرْسَلْنَآ

اِلٰى فِرْعَوْنَ رَسُوْلًا

٢. اَمَّنْ هٰذَا الَّذِيْ هُوَ جُنْدٌ لَّكُمْ يَنْصُرُكُمْ مِنْ دُوْنِ

الرَّحْمٰنِ اِنِ الْكَافِرُوْنَ اِلَّا فِيْ غُرُوْرٍ

٣. بِسْمِ اللهِ الرَّحْمٰنِ الرَّحِيْمِ هَلْ اَتٰى عَلَى الْاِنْسَانِ

حِيْنٌ مِّنَ الدَّهْرِ لَمْ يَكُنْ شَيْئًا مَّذْكُوْرًا

24

4. قُلْ اَرَءَيْتُمْ اِنْ اَهْلَكَنِيَ اللهُ وَمَنْ مَّعِيَ اَوْ رَحِمَنَا فَمَنْ يُّجِيْرُ الْكَافِرِيْنَ مِنْ عَذَابٍ اَلِيْمٍ

5. وَاِنْ يَّكَادُ الَّذِيْنَ كَفَرُوْا لَيُزْلِقُوْنَكَ بِاَبْصَارِهِمْ لَمَّا سَمِعُوا الذِّكْرَ وَيَقُوْلُوْنَ اِنَّهٗ لَمَجْنُوْنٌ

6. قَالُوْا بَلٰى قَدْ جَاءَنَا نَذِيْرٌ فَكَذَّبْنَا وَقُلْنَا مَا نَزَّلَ اللهُ مِنْ شَيْءٍ اِنْ اَنْتُمْ اِلَّا فِيْ ضَلَالٍ كَبِيْرٍ

7. اِنَّ الَّذِيْنَ اٰمَنُوْا وَعَمِلُوا الصّٰلِحٰتِ لَهُمْ جَنّٰتٌ تَجْرِيْ مِنْ تَحْتِهَا الْاَنْهٰرُ ذٰلِكَ الْفَوْزُ الْكَبِيْرُ

8. اِنَّاۤ اَنْذَرْنٰكُمْ عَذَابًا قَرِيْبًا يَّوْمَ يَنْظُرُ الْمَرْءُ مَا قَدَّمَتْ يَدٰهُ وَيَقُوْلُ الْكَافِرُ يٰلَيْتَنِيْ كُنْتُ تُرَابًا

THE MAKHRAJ OF THE HUROOF NIT'EE نِطْعِيّ

A *nit'ee* letter is one that is produced by making the tip of the tongue touch the gums behind the front teeth. The

letters ت, د and ط are all *nit'ee* letters.

Examples: اَطُ اَدْ اَتُ

EXERCISE

Underline all the huroof Nit'ee in the verses below, and then read them.

١. اِذْ نَادٰىهُ رَبُّهُ بِالْوَادِ الْمُقَدَّسِ طُوًى

٢. وَاَنَّا مِنَّا الصّٰلِحُوْنَ وَمِنَّا دُوْنَ ذٰلِكَ كُنَّا طَرَآئِقَ قِدَدًا

٣. وَاَنَّهُ لَمَّا قَامَ عَبْدُ اللهِ يَدْعُوْهُ كَادُوْا يَكُوْنُوْنَ عَلَيْهِ لِبَدًا

٤. نَحْنُ خَلَقْنٰهُمْ وَشَدَدْنَآ اَسْرَهُمْ وَاِذَا شِئْنَا بَدَّلْنَآ اَمْثَالَهُمْ تَبْدِيْلًا

5. وَاَنَّا لَا نَدْرِي اَشَرٌّ اُرِيدَ بِمَنْ فِي الْاَرْضِ اَمْ اَرَادَ بِهِمْ رَبُّهُمْ رَشَدًا

6. مِمَّا خَطِيْٓئٰتِهِمْ اُغْرِقُوْا فَاُدْخِلُوْا نَارًا فَلَمْ يَجِدُوْا لَهُمْ مِنْ دُوْنِ اللّٰهِ اَنْصَارًا

7. لِيَعْلَمَ اَنْ قَدْ اَبْلَغُوْا رِسٰلٰتِ رَبِّهِمْ وَاَحَاطَ بِمَا لَدَيْهِمْ وَاَحْصٰى كُلَّ شَيْءٍ عَدَدًا

THE MAKHRAJ OF THE HUROOF THANAWI ثَنَوِيّ

A *thanawi* letter is one that is produced by making the front of the tongue come out of the mouth and touch the edges of

the teeth. The letters ث, ذ and ظ, are *thanawi* letters.

Examples: اَظْ اَذْ اَثْ

EXERCISE

Underline all the huroof thanawi in the verses below, and then read them.

١. اِنْطَلِقُوْٓا اِلٰى ظِلٍّ ذِيْ ثَلٰثِ شُعَبٍ

٢. فَيَوْمَئِذٍ لَّا يُعَذِّبُ عَذَابَهٗٓ اَحَدٌ

٣. ثُمَّ يُقَالُ هٰذَا الَّذِيْ كُنْتُمْ بِهٖ تُكَذِّبُوْنَ

٤. ثُمَّ فِيْ سِلْسِلَةٍ ذَرْعُهَا سَبْعُوْنَ ذِرَاعًا فَاسْلُكُوْهُ

٥. وَدَانِيَةً عَلَيْهِمْ ظِلَالُهَا وَذُلِّلَتْ قُطُوْفُهَا تَذْلِيْلًا

٦. وَاَنَّهُمْ ظَنُّوْا كَمَا ظَنَنْتُمْ اَنْ لَّنْ يَّبْعَثَ اللّٰهُ اَحَدًا

28

THE MAKHRAJ OF THE HUROOF SAFEER صَفِير

A *safeer* letter is one that is produced by making the front edges of the tongue touch or nearly touch the edges of both the top teeth and bottom teeth, and at the same time, make a whistling sound.

The letters ز, س and ص are all *safeer* letters.

Examples: اَزْ اَسْ اَصْ

EXERCISE

Underline all the huroof safeer in the verses below, and then read them.

١. فَسَوْفَ يُحَاسَبُ حِسَابًا يَّسِيْرًا

٢. اَلَّذِيْ يُوَسْوِسُ فِيْ صُدُوْرِ النَّاسِ

٣. وَيُسْقَوْنَ فِيْهَا كَأْسًا كَانَ مِزَاجُهَا زَنْجَبِيْلًا

٤. ثُمَّ فِيْ سِلْسِلَةٍ ذَرْعُهَا سَبْعُوْنَ ذِرَاعًا فَاسْلُكُوْهُ

٥. اِذَا زُلْزِلَتِ الْاَرْضُ زِلْزَالَهَا

29

THE MAKHRAJ OF THE HUROOF SHAFAWII شَفَوِيّ

A *shafawii* letter is one that is made using the lips.

The letters ف, ب, م and و *ghayr maddah* are all *shafawii*.

1. ف is made by curling out the lower lip and making its inner portion touch the edge of the upper teeth.

    Example: أَفْ

2. ب is made by joining the inner lips together.

    Example: أَبْ

3. م is made by joining the outer lips together.

    Example: أَمْ

4. و *ghayr maddah* is made by joining the ends, and not the middle of the lips.

    Example: أَوْ

Note: any و saakin (وْ) that doesn't have a *pesh* before it is called و *ghayr maddah*.

EXERCISE

Underline & read all the huroof shafawii in the verses below.

١. فَبَشِّرْهُمْ بِعَذَابٍ أَلِيمٍ

٢. فَسَبِّحْ بِاسْمِ رَبِّكَ الْعَظِيمِ

٣. فَمَا تَنْفَعُهُمْ شَفَاعَةُ الشَّافِعِينَ

٤. اَلسَّمَاءُ مُنْفَطِرٌ بِهِ كَانَ وَعْدُهُ مَفْعُولًا

٥. كَلَّا إِنَّهُمْ عَنْ رَبِّهِمْ يَوْمَئِذٍ لَّمَحْجُوبُونَ

٦. خِتَامُهُ مِسْكٌ وَّفِي ذَلِكَ فَلْيَتَنَافَسِ الْمُتَنَافِسُونَ

٧. وَلَقَدْ كَذَّبَ الَّذِينَ مِنْ قَبْلِهِمْ فَكَيْفَ كَانَ نَكِيرِ

٨. اَلَمْ تَرَ كَيْفَ فَعَلَ رَبُّكَ بِأَصْحَبِ الْفِيلِ

٩. تَبَّتْ يَدَا أَبِي لَهَبٍ وَّتَبَّ

THE MAKHRAJ OF THE HUROOF GHUNNA غُنَّة

A *ghunna* letter is made by taking the sound up to the bony part of the nose. There are 2 ghunna letters:

م - Example: عَمَّ

ن - Example: اِنَّ

EXERCISE

Underline & read all the huroof ghunna in the verses below.

١. هَمَّازٍ مَّشَّآءٍ بِنَمِيمٍ

٢. كَلَّا اِنَّا خَلَقْنٰهُمْ مِّمَّا يَعْلَمُوْنَ

٣. ثُمَّ لَتُسْئَلُنَّ يَوْمَئِذٍ عَنِ النَّعِيْمِ

٤. اِنَّا هَدَيْنٰهُ السَّبِيْلَ اِمَّا شَاكِرًا وَّاِمَّا كَفُوْرًا

٥. وَاَنَّا مِنَّا الصّٰلِحُوْنَ وَمِنَّا دُوْنَ ذٰلِكَ كُنَّا طَرَآئِقَ قِدَدًا

٦. وَاَنَّا ظَنَنَّآ اَنْ لَّنْ تَقُوْلَ الْاِنْسُ وَالْجِنُّ عَلَى اللهِ كَذِبًا

32

1.4 -IMPORTANT TERMS USED THROUGHOUT THIS BOOK TO DESCRIBE THE WRITING OF ARABIC

HARAKAAT حَرَكَاتْ

Harakat	These 3 symbols (*zabar – zer - pesh*) are each a harakat. In Arabic, they are called *fatha*, *kasra* and *damma*.
Mutaharrik	When a *harakat* appears on a letter, the letter is said to be *mutaharrik*.

All 3 letters in the word كُتِبَ are *mutaharrik*.

TANWEEN تَنْوِيْن

tanween	These 3 symbols (which are doublings of the previous 3 symbols) are called *tanween*. They change the sound into a noon saakin (نْ).
Munawwan	A letter with a *tanween* on is called a *munawwan* letter.

SUKOON سُكُوْن

Sukoon	The symbol ْ is called *sukoon*
Saakin	A letter with a *sukoon* on is called a *saakin* letter

TASHDEED تَشْدِيد

Shaddah	The symbol ّ is called *shaddah*
Mushaddad	A letter with a *shaddah* on is a *mushaddad* letter

WAQF وَقْف

Waqf	This means to stop reading at the end of a word, by breathing in.
Mawqoof	The letter that you stop reading on is the mawqoof letter.

example: قُلْ هُوَ اللهُ اَحَدٌ ← قُلْ هُوَ اللهُ اَحَدْ.

GHUNNAH غُنَّة

Ghunnah	Any letter that is read by taking it into the nose is a ghunnah letter.
Haddul ghunnah	The amount of time that a ghunnah continues for is about one *alif*.
Alif	An *alif* is equal to the length of time it takes to open a closed finger or close an open finger (around one second).

Example: اِنْ كُنْتُمْ مُّؤْمِنِينَ

IKHFAA اِخْفَاءٌ

To transfer part of the *makhraj* of a ن or م to the nose, is called *ikhfaa*.

Example: مِنْ قَبْلُ

QALB / IQLAAB قَلْب /اِقْلَاب

Reading one letter instead of another is called *qalb* or *iqlaab*.

Example: مِنْۢ بَعْدِي and عَلِيمٌ ۢبِذَاتِ الصُّدُوْر

IDHGHAAM اِدْغَامٌ

To join a saakin letter with a following tashdeed letter and to then read the saakin letter like the following one is called *idhghaam*.

Examples: مَنْ يُّؤْمِن - قَدْ تَّبَيَّنَ

IZHAAR اِظْهَارٌ

To read a letter without any trace of *idhghaam* or *ghunna* is called *izhaar*.

Examples: وَانْحَرْ - اَنْعَمْتَ عَلَيْهِمْ

You will learn the rules of *idhghaam*, *izhaar*, *qalb* and *ikhfaa* in detail later on, inshallah.

35

1.5 - LETTERS WITH A MOUTH FULL OF AIR, AND EMPTY OF AIR

FULL MOUTH LETTERS - ISTI'LAAII اِسْتِعْلَائِيّ

There are 7 full mouth letters. They are:

خ ص ض ط ظ   غ   ق

These 7 letters are read with a mouth full of air. When reading them, the back end of the tongue is raised up and touches the far end of the hard palate.

Example: the ق in قَالَ

EXERCISE

Underline & read all the full mouth letters in the verses below

1. فَلَا صَدَّقَ وَلَا صَلَّى

2. ثُمَّ شَقَقْنَا الْاَرْضَ شَقًّا

3. وَمِنْ شَرِّ غَاسِقٍ اِذَا وَقَبَ

4. نِصْفَهُ اَوِ انْقُصْ مِنْهُ قَلِيْلًا

5. قَوَارِيْرَ مِنْ فِضَّةٍ قَدَّرُوْهَا تَقْدِيْرًا

36

6. لَقَدْ خَلَقْنَا الْاِنْسَانَ فِيْ اَحْسَنِ تَقْوِيْمٍ

7. فَقُلْتُ اسْتَغْفِرُوْا رَبَّكُمْ اِنَّهُ كَانَ غَفَّارًا

8. فَقَالَ لَهُمْ رَسُوْلُ اللّٰهِ نَاقَةَ اللّٰهِ وَسُقْيٰهَا

9. ثُمَّ ارْجِعِ الْبَصَرَ كَرَّتَيْنِ يَنْقَلِبْ اِلَيْكَ الْبَصَرُ خَاسِئًا وَّهُوَ حَسِيْرٌ

10. وَاَنَّا مِنَّا الصّٰلِحُوْنَ وَمِنَّا دُوْنَ ذٰلِكَ كُنَّا طَرَآئِقَ قِدَدًا

11. صِرَاطَ الَّذِيْنَ اَنْعَمْتَ عَلَيْهِمْ غَيْرِ الْمَغْضُوْبِ عَلَيْهِمْ وَلَا الضَّآلِّيْنَ

12. خَاشِعَةً اَبْصَارُهُمْ تَرْهَقُهُمْ ذِلَّةٌ وَّقَدْ كَانُوْا يُدْعَوْنَ اِلَى السُّجُوْدِ وَهُمْ سٰلِمُوْنَ

١٣. وَاَنْ لَّوِ اسْتَقَامُوْا عَلَى الطَّرِيْقَةِ لَاَسْقَيْنٰهُمْ مَّاءً غَدَقًا

١٤. اِنَّا بَلَوْنٰهُمْ كَمَا بَلَوْنَاۤ اَصْحٰبَ الْجَنَّةِ اِذْ اَقْسَمُوْا

لَيَصْرِمُنَّهَا مُصْبِحِيْنَ

١٥. اِلَّا الَّذِيْنَ اٰمَنُوْا وَعَمِلُوا الصّٰلِحٰتِ وَتَوَاصَوْا بِالْحَقِّ

وَتَوَاصَوْا بِالصَّبْرِ

١٦. مِمَّا خَطِيْٓئٰتِهِمْ اُغْرِقُوْا فَاُدْخِلُوْا نَارًا فَلَمْ يَجِدُوْا لَهُمْ

مِّنْ دُوْنِ اللّٰهِ اَنْصَارًا

١٧. اَلَّذِيْ خَلَقَ سَبْعَ سَمٰوٰتٍ طِبَاقًا مَّا تَرٰى فِيْ خَلْقِ

الرَّحْمٰنِ مِنْ تَفٰوُتٍ فَارْجِعِ الْبَصَرَ هَلْ تَرٰى مِنْ فُطُوْرٍ

١٨. وَوَضَعْنَا عَنْكَ وِزْرَكَ ٠ الَّذِيْۤ اَنْقَضَ ظَهْرَكَ ٠

EMPTY MOUTH LETTERS اِسْتِفَالِيٌّ

The remaining 22 letters are empty mouth letters. When reading them, the back end of the tongue does NOT touch the hard palate, and the mouth does not fill up with air.

Example: the ذ in ذٰلِكَ

EXERCISE

Underline the empty mouth letters below & read the verses:

ثُمَّ عَبَسَ وَبَسَرَۙ وَجَنّٰتٍ اَلْفَافًاۙ حَدَآئِقَ وَاَعْنَابًاۙ

وَكَوَاعِبَ اَتْرَابًاۙ وَزَيْتُوْنًا وَّنَخْلًاۙ مُطَاعٍ ثَمَّ اَمِيْنٍۙ

وَمَا هُوَ بِالْهَزْلِۙ وَوَالِدٍ وَّمَا وَلَدَۙ لَتَرَوُنَّ الْجَحِيْمَۙ

مٰلِكِ يَوْمِ الدِّيْنِۙ وَصَاحِبَتِهٖ وَاَخِيْهِۙ فَقُتِلَ كَيْفَ

قَدَّرَۙ فَالْعٰصِفٰتِ عَصْفًاۙ وَالنّٰشِرٰتِ نَشْرًاۙ فَالْفٰرِقٰتِ

فَرْقًاۙ اِلٰى قَدَرٍ مَّعْلُوْمٍۙ وَالْجِبَالَ اَوْتَادًاۙ وَالنّٰشِطٰتِ

نَشْطًاۙ مِّمَّا خَطِيْئٰتِهِمْ اُغْرِقُوْا فَاُدْخِلُوْا نَارًا فَلَمْ يَجِدُوْا

لَهُمْ مِّنْ دُوْنِ اللّٰهِ اَنْصَارًاۙ

39

HUROOF MUSHTARAK (MIXED STATE LETTERS) مُشْتَرَكْ

The 4 letters (اَ) الف مدة, (وُ) واو مدة, ل and ر are sometimes spoken with a mouth full of air, and sometimes with a mouth empty of air.

ALIF MADDA AND WOW MADDAH اَلِفْ مَدَّةٌ وَ وَاوْ مَدَّةٌ

الف مدة and واو مدة : If these 2 letters come after a full mouth letter, they too will be read with a mouth full of air.

examples: قَالَ and قُوْلُوْ

If, however, they come after an empty mouth letter, they too will be read with a mouth empty of air.

examples: سَمِعُوْا and رَبَّنَا

EXERCISE

Underline all the *alif maddah*s and *wow maddah*s in the verses below and then read the verses.

1. وَيَقُوْلُوْنَ مَتٰى هٰذَا الْوَعْدُ اِنْ كُنْتُمْ صٰدِقِيْنَ

2. فَلَاۤ اُقْسِمُ بِرَبِّ الْمَشْرِقِ وَالْمَغْرِبِ اِنَّا لَقٰدِرُوْنَ

40

3. مِّمَّا خَطِيئَٰتِهِمْ أُغْرِقُوا فَأُدْخِلُوا نَارًا فَلَمْ يَجِدُوا لَهُم مِّن دُوْنِ اللّٰهِ أَنْصَارًا

4. وَقَالُوا لَا تَذَرُنَّ اٰلِهَتَكُمْ وَلَا تَذَرُنَّ وَدًّا وَّلَا سُوَاعًا وَّلَا يَغُوثَ وَيَعُوقَ وَنَسْرًا

5. يَوْمَ يَقُوْمُ الرُّوْحُ وَالْمَلَٰئِكَةُ صَفًّا لَّا يَتَكَلَّمُوْنَ إِلَّا مَنْ أَذِنَ لَهُ الرَّحْمٰنُ وَقَالَ صَوَابًا

6. وَإِنْ يَّكَادُ الَّذِيْنَ كَفَرُوا لَيُزْلِقُوْنَكَ بِأَبْصَارِهِمْ لَمَّا سَمِعُوا الذِّكْرَ وَيَقُوْلُوْنَ إِنَّهُ لَمَجْنُوْنٌ

LAAM IN THE WORD ALLAH اَللّٰه

When ل is in the word اللّٰه, the word اللّٰه will be spoken with a mouth full of air if there is a *zabar* or *pesh* immediately before the ل.

Examples: أَرَادَ اللّٰهُ and يَشَآءُ اللّٰهُ

If, however, there is a *zer* (*kasrah*) immediately before it, then it is spoken with a mouth empty of air.

example: بِسْمِ اللّٰهِ

EXERCISE

1. Underline the word اللّٰه in the verses below.
2. Write *f* underneath if it is full mouth.
3. Write *e* underneath if it is empty mouth.

1. بِسْمِ اللّٰهِ الرَّحْمٰنِ الرَّحِيمِ يَآ اَيُّهَا الَّذِيْنَ اٰمَنُوْا لَا تُقَدِّمُوْا بَيْنَ يَدَيِ اللّٰهِ وَرَسُوْلِهٖ وَاتَّقُوا اللّٰهَ اِنَّ اللّٰهَ سَمِيْعٌ عَلِيْمٌ

42

٢. قَدْ سَمِعَ اللهُ قَوْلَ الَّتِي تُجَادِلُكَ فِي زَوْجِهَا وَتَشْتَكِيٓ إِلَى اللهِ وَاللهُ يَسْمَعُ تَحَاوُرَكُمَآ إِنَّ اللهَ سَمِيعٌۢ بَصِيرٌ

٣. إِذَا جَآءَكَ الْمُنَافِقُوْنَ قَالُوْا نَشْهَدُ إِنَّكَ لَرَسُوْلُ اللهِ وَاللهُ يَعْلَمُ إِنَّكَ لَرَسُوْلُهٗ

٤. أَجَعَلْتُمْ سِقَايَةَ الْحَآجِّ وَعِمَارَةَ الْمَسْجِدِ الْحَرَامِ كَمَنْ اٰمَنَ بِاللهِ وَالْيَوْمِ الْاٰخِرِ وَجَاهَدَ فِي سَبِيْلِ اللهِ لَا يَسْتَوُوْنَ عِنْدَ اللهِ وَاللهُ لَا يَهْدِى الْقَوْمَ الظّٰلِمِيْنَ

٥. وَمِنَ الْاَعْرَابِ مَنْ يُّؤْمِنُ بِاللهِ وَالْيَوْمِ الْاٰخِرِ وَيَتَّخِذُ مَا يُنْفِقُ قُرُبٰتٍ عِنْدَ اللهِ وَصَلَوٰتِ الرَّسُوْلِ اَلَآ إِنَّهَا قُرْبَةٌ لَّهُمْ سَيُدْخِلُهُمُ اللهُ فِيْ رَحْمَتِهٖ إِنَّ اللهَ غَفُوْرٌ رَّحِيْمٌ

٤٣

THE LETTER RAA راء

There are 5 rules for the letter raa (راء)

1) راء mutaharrik

2) راء mushaddad

3) راء saakin

4) راء saakin waqfii

5) راء mawqoof

RAA MUTAHARRIK رَاء مُتَحَرِّك

1) A رَاء mutaharrik is a رَاء with a *zabar*, *zer* or *pesh* on it.

A رَاء mutaharrik with a *zabar* or *pesh* above it is prayed with a mouth full of air.

Examples: رَبَّمَا and رُبَّكَ.

A رَاء with a *zer* is prayed with a mouth empty of air.

Examples: رِجَال

EXERCISE

1. Underline each *raa mutaharrik*
2. write *f* (full of air) or *e* (empty of air) under each *raa mutaharrik*
3. read the verses correctly.

1. فَلَا أُقْسِمُ بِرَبِّ الْمَشْرِقِ وَالْمَغْرِبِ إِنَّا لَقَادِرُونَ

2. فَأَمَّا الْإِنْسَانُ إِذَا مَا ابْتَلَاهُ رَبُّهُ فَأَكْرَمَهُ وَنَعَّمَهُ فَيَقُولُ رَبِّي أَكْرَمَنِ

٣. عٰلِيَهُمْ ثِيَابُ سُنْدُسٍ خُضْرٌ وَّاِسْتَبْرَقٌ وَّحُلُّوٓا اَسَاوِرَ مِنْ فِضَّةٍ وَّسَقٰهُمْ رَبُّهُمْ شَرَابًا طَهُوْرًا

٤. اِنَّ الَّذِيْنَ كَفَرُوْا مِنْ اَهْلِ الْكِتٰبِ وَالْمُشْرِكِيْنَ فِيْ نَارِ جَهَنَّمَ خٰلِدِيْنَ فِيْهَا

٥. جَزَآؤُهُمْ عِنْدَ رَبِّهِمْ جَنّٰتُ عَدْنٍ تَجْرِيْ مِنْ تَحْتِهَا الْاَنْهٰرُ خٰلِدِيْنَ فِيْهَآ اَبَدًا رَّضِيَ اللهُ عَنْهُمْ وَرَضُوْا عَنْهُ ذٰلِكَ لِمَنْ خَشِيَ رَبَّهٗ

٦. وَلِيَقُوْلَ الَّذِيْنَ فِيْ قُلُوْبِهِمْ مَّرَضٌ وَّالْكٰفِرُوْنَ مَاذَآ اَرَادَ اللهُ بِهٰذَا مَثَلًا كَذٰلِكَ يُضِلُّ اللهُ مَنْ يَّشَآءُ وَيَهْدِيْ مَنْ يَّشَآءُ وَمَا يَعْلَمُ جُنُوْدَ رَبِّكَ اِلَّا هُوَ وَمَا هِيَ اِلَّا ذِكْرٰى لِلْبَشَرِ

RAA MUSHADDAD رَاء مُشَدَّدُ

2) A رَاء mushaddad is a رَاء with a *tashdeed* on it.

A رَاء mushaddad with a *zabar* or *pesh* on it is prayed with a mouth full of air.

Examples: شَرًّا يَّرَه and فَفِرُّوا

A رَاء mushaddad with a zer is prayed with a mouth empty of air.

Examples: دُرِّيُّ

EXERCISE

1. Underline each *raa mushaddad*
2. write *f* (full of air) or *e* (empty of air) under each *raa mushaddad*
3. read the verses correctly.

1. وَقَالَ الَّذِيْنَ اتَّبَعُوْا لَوْ اَنَّ لَنَا كَرَّةً فَنَتَبَرَّاَ مِنْهُمْ كَمَا تَبَرَّءُوْا مِنَّا كَذٰلِكَ يُرِيْهِمُ اللهُ اَعْمَالَهُمْ حَسَرٰتٍ عَلَيْهِمْ وَمَا هُمْ بِخٰرِجِيْنَ مِنَ النَّارِ

47

٢. اِنَّمَا حَرَّمَ عَلَيْكُمُ الْمَيْتَةَ وَالدَّمَ وَلَحْمَ الْخِنْزِيرِ وَمَآ
اُهِلَّ بِهٖ لِغَيْرِ اللهِ فَمَنِ اضْطُرَّ غَيْرَ بَاغٍ وَّلَا عَادٍ فَلَآ اِثْمَ
عَلَيْهِ اِنَّ اللهَ غَفُوْرٌ رَّحِيْمٌ

٣. وَمَآ اَرْسَلْنَا مِنْ رَّسُوْلٍ اِلَّا لِيُطَاعَ بِاِذْنِ اللهِ وَلَوْ اَنَّهُمْ
اِذْ ظَّلَمُوْٓا اَنْفُسَهُمْ جَآءُوْكَ فَاسْتَغْفَرُوا اللهَ وَاسْتَغْفَرَ
لَهُمُ الرَّسُوْلُ لَوَجَدُوا اللهَ تَوَّابًا رَّحِيْمًا

٤. وَاِذَا مَسَّ الْاِنْسَانَ الضُّرُّ دَعَانَا لِجَنْبِهٖٓ اَوْ قَاعِدًا اَوْ
قَآئِمًا فَلَمَّا كَشَفْنَا عَنْهُ ضُرَّهٗ مَرَّ كَاَنْ لَّمْ يَدْعُنَآ اِلٰى ضُرٍّ
مَّسَّهٗ كَذٰلِكَ زُيِّنَ لِلْمُسْرِفِيْنَ مَا كَانُوْا يَعْمَلُوْنَ

RAA SAAKIN رَاءْ سَاكِنْ

3) A رَاءْ saakin is a رَاءْ with a sukoon on it, for example رُ

a) A رَاءْ saakin with a *zabar* or *pesh before* it is prayed with a mouth full of air.

Examples: مُرْسَلِيْنَ and بَرْقٌ

b) A رَاءْ saakin with a *zer before* it is prayed with a mouth empty of air.

Examples: فِرْعَوْنَ

However, there are 3 additional conditions that must be met if a رَاءْ saakin with a *zer before* is to be prayed with a mouth empty of air:

i) The *zer* in the letter before the رَاءْ saakin must be an *asli* one (a permanent letter of the word) and not a temporary one. If it is a temporary one, the رَاءْ saakin must be spoken with a mouth full of air.

example: اِرْجِعِيْ

49

ii) the راء saakin and the letter with the *zer* on it must be in the same word. If they are in separate words, the راء saakin will be spoken with a mouth full of air.

example: لِمَنِ ارْتَضٰى

iii) There must be an empty mouth letter after the راء saakin. If, instead, there is a full mouth letter after the راء saakin, it must be spoken with a mouth full of air.

example: لَبِالْمِرْصَاد

EXERCISE

1. Underline each *raa saakin*
2. write *f* (full of air) or *e* (empty of air) under each *raa saakin*
3. read the verses correctly.

1. اِنَّا مُرْسِلُو النَّاقَةِ فِتْنَةً لَّهُمْ فَارْتَقِبْهُمْ وَاصْطَبِرْ

2. وَاِنِّيْ مُرْسِلَةٌ اِلَيْهِمْ بِهَدِيَّةٍ فَنَاظِرَةٌ بِمَ يَرْجِعُ الْمُرْسَلُوْنَ

٣. اِلٰى فِرْعَوْنَ وَمَلَئِهٖ فَاتَّبَعُوْٓا اَمْرَ فِرْعَوْنَ وَمَآ اَمْرُ
فِرْعَوْنَ بِرَشِيْدٍ

٤. يٰٓاَيُّهَا الَّذِيْنَ اٰمَنُوْٓا اِنْ تَتَّقُوا اللّٰهَ يَجْعَلْ لَّكُمْ
فُرْقَانًا وَّيُكَفِّرْ عَنْكُمْ سَيِّاٰتِكُمْ وَيَغْفِرْ لَكُمْ وَاللّٰهُ ذُو
الْفَضْلِ الْعَظِيْمِ

٥. فَمَآ اٰمَنَ لِمُوْسٰٓى اِلَّا ذُرِّيَّةٌ مِّنْ قَوْمِهٖ عَلٰى خَوْفٍ مِّنْ
فِرْعَوْنَ وَمَلَاۡئِهِمْ اَنْ يَّفْتِنَهُمْ وَاِنَّ فِرْعَوْنَ لَعَالٍ فِي
الْاَرْضِ وَاِنَّهٗ لَمِنَ الْمُسْرِفِيْنَ

٦. اِسْتَغْفِرْ لَهُمْ اَوْ لَا تَسْتَغْفِرْ لَهُمْ اِنْ تَسْتَغْفِرْ لَهُمْ
سَبْعِيْنَ مَرَّةً فَلَنْ يَّغْفِرَ اللّٰهُ لَهُمْ

٧. وَلَا يَرْضٰى لِعِبَادِهِ الْكُفْرَ وَاِنْ تَشْكُرُوْا يَرْضَهُ لَكُمْ

RAA SAAKIN WAQFII رَاء سَاكِنْ وَقْفِيْ

4) A رَاء saakin waqfii is a رَاء saakin that was originally mutaharrik but became saakin because it was the last letter in the last word of an ayah.

If a رَاء saakin waqfii has a letter that is mutaharrik with a

pesh or zabar before it then the رَاء saakin waqfii will be read with a mouth full of air.

examples: بِقَدَرٌ ➡ بِقَدَرٍۣ

وَسُعُرٌ ➡ وَسُعُرٍۣ

If a رَاء saakin waqfii has a letter that is mutaharrik with a

zer before it then the رَاء saakin waqfii will be read with a mouth empty of air.

example: مُنْتَصِرٌ ➡ مُنْتَصِرٍۣ

EXERCISE – READ THE EXAMPLES BELOW
1. Underline each raa saakin waqfii
2. write *f* (full of air) or *e* (empty of air) under each one & read

ثُمَّ نَظَرَ۟ كَلَّا لَا وَزَرَ۟ سَاُصْلِيْهِ سَقَرَ۟ وَخَسَفَ الْقَمَرُ۟

نَذِيرًا لِّلْبَشَرِ۞ ثُمَّ عَبَسَ وَبَسَرَ۞ لَوَّاحَةٌ لِّلْبَشَرِ۞ لَا

تُبْقِي وَلَا تَذَرُ۞ فَإِذَا بَرِقَ الْبَصَرُ۞ إِنَّهُ فَكَّرَ وَقَدَّرَ۞

عَلَيْهَا تِسْعَةَ عَشَرَ۞ مَا سَلَكَكُمْ فِي سَقَرَ۞ وَلَا تَمْنُنْ

تَسْتَكْثِرُ۞ وَمَآ أَدْرَاكَ مَا سَقَرُ۞ وَالصُّبْحِ إِذَآ أَسْفَرَ۞

يَوْمَ تُبْلَى السَّرَائِرُ۞ إِنَّهَا لَإِحْدَى الْكُبَرِ۞ إِلَّا مَن تَوَلَّى

وَكَفَرَ۞ حَتَّى زُرْتُمُ الْمَقَابِرَ۞ وَجُمِعَ الشَّمْسُ وَالْقَمَرُ۞

لَسْتَ عَلَيْهِم بِمُصَيْطِرٍ۞ إِنَّهُ عَلَى رَجْعِهِ لَقَادِرٌ۞ إِنَّ

شَانِئَكَ هُوَ الْأَبْتَرُ۞ إِنْ هَذَآ إِلَّا قَوْلُ الْبَشَرِ۞ فَذَكِّرْ إِنَّمَآ

أَنتَ مُذَكِّرٌ۞ فَمَالَهُ مِن قُوَّةٍ وَّلَا نَاصِرٍ۞ فَقَالَ إِنْ هَذَآ إِلَّا

سِحْرٌ يُؤْثَرُ۞ فَيُعَذِّبُهُ اللهُ الْعَذَابَ الْأَ كْبَرَ۞ إِنَّآ

أَعْطَيْنَاكَ الْكَوْثَرَ۞ يَآ أَيُّهَا الْمُدَّثِّرُ۞

RAA MAWQOOF رَاءٌ مَوْقُوْفٌ

5) A رَاء *mawqoof* is a رَاء *mutaharrik* that has become رَاء *saakin* because it is at the end of a verse, **and** the letter before it is also a *saakin* letter.

If there is a يَاء *saakin* before a رَاء *mawqoof* then the رَاء *mawqoof* will always be prayed with a mouth empty of air.

example: خَيْرٌ ۝ and بَصِيْرٌ ۝

If there is any other saakin letter before the رَاء *mawqoof* and the letter before these two letters has a *zabar* or *pesh*, then the رَاء *mawqoof* will be prayed with a full mouth.

Examples: وَتَوَاصَوْا بِالصَّبْرِ ۝ and مَا فِي الصُّدُوْرِ ۝

And if the 3rd to last letter is a zer (ِ) then the رُ is read with an empty mouth.

example: ذِي الذِّكْرِ ۝

EXERCISE
1. Underline each *raa mawqoof*
2. write *f* (full of air) or *e* (empty of air) under each one
3. read the verses correctly.
4. One verse does not have a *raa mawqoof*. Find & underline it.

وَحُصِّلَ مَا فِي الصُّدُورِ ۞ فَاِذَا نُقِرَ فِي النَّاقُورِ ۞ اِنَّهُ ظَنَّ

اَنْ لَّنْ يَّحُورَ ۞ فَذٰلِكَ يَوْمَئِذٍ يَّوْمٌ عَسِيرٌ ۞ عَلَى

الْكَافِرِينَ غَيْرُ يَسِيرٍ ۞ فَاعْتَرَفُوْا بِذَنْبِهِمْ فَسُحْقًا

لِّاَصْحَابِ السَّعِيرِ ۞ اِذَاۤ اُلْقُوْا فِيهَا سَمِعُوْا لَهَا شَهِيقًا وَّهِيَ

تَفُوْرُ ۞ كَاَنَّهُ جِمٰلَتٌ صُفْرٌ ۞ فَصَلِّ لِرَبِّكَ وَانْحَرْ ۞ اِنَّ

الْاِنْسَانَ لَفِي خُسْرٍ ۞ هَلْ فِي ذٰلِكَ قَسَمٌ لِّذِي حِجْرٍ ۞

اِنَّهَا تَرْمِي بِشَرَرٍ كَالْقَصْرِ ۞ وَمَاۤ اَدْرٰىكَ مَا لَيْلَةُ الْقَدْرِ ۞

سَلَامٌ هِيَ حَتّٰى مَطْلَعِ الْفَجْرِ ۞ لَيْلَةُ الْقَدْرِ خَيْرٌ مِّنْ اَلْفِ

شَهْرٍ ۞ وَالْعَصْرِ ۞ تَنَزَّلُ الْمَلٰٓئِكَةُ وَالرُّوحُ فِيهَا بِاِذْنِ

رَبِّهِمْ مِّنْ كُلِّ اَمْرٍ ۞ اِنَّاۤ اَنْزَلْنَاهُ فِي لَيْلَةِ الْقَدْرِ ۞

وَالْفَجْرِ ۞ وَلَيَالٍ عَشْرٍ ۞ وَالشَّفْعِ وَالْوَتْرِ ۞ وَالَّيْلِ اِذَا

يَسْرِ ۞ هَلْ فِي ذٰلِكَ قَسَمٌ لِّذِي حِجْرٍ ۞

55

1.6.1: THE RULES OF NOON SAAKIN AND TANWEEN نُوْنُ سَاكِنٍ وَالتَّنْوِيْنُ

A ن *saakin* is a ن with a *sukoon*.

Example: اِنْ

Tanween is 2 zabars, 2 zers or 2 peshes.

Examples: نَاصِبَةٌ اٰنِيَةٍ حَامِيَةً

There are 4 rules for ن *saakin* and tanween.

1)   Izhaar
2)   Idghaam
3)   Iqlaab
4)   Ikhfaa

IZHAAR اِظْهَارُ

1) *Izhaar* - There will be *izhaar* when there is a *huroof halqi*

after a ن *saakin* or *tanween*. This *Izhaar* is called *Izhaar halqi*. Izhaar means no ghunna is done.

example: مَنْ اٰمَنَ and حَكِيْمٌ عَلِيْمٌ

Note: The *huroof halqi* are خ غ ح ع ﻫ ء

56

EXERCISE

Underline all the *izhaar* occurrences in the verses below and read them

١. اِذْ نَادٰى رَبَّهٗ نِدَآءً خَفِيًّا

٢. جَزَآءً مِّنْ رَّبِّكَ عَطَآءً حِسَابًا

٣. فَمِنْهُمْ مَّنْ اٰمَنَ بِهٖ وَمِنْهُمْ مَّنْ صَدَّ عَنْهُ وَكَفٰى بِجَهَنَّمَ سَعِيْرًا

٤. وَمِنْهُمْ مَّنْ عٰهَدَ اللهَ لَئِنْ اٰتٰىنَا مِنْ فَضْلِهٖ لَنَصَّدَّقَنَّ وَلَنَكُوْنَنَّ مِنَ الصّٰلِحِيْنَ

٥. فَسَخَّرْنَا لَهُ الرِّيْحَ تَجْرِيْ بِاَمْرِهٖ رُخَآءً حَيْثُ اَصَابَ

٦. قُلْ اَرَءَيْتُمْ اِنْ كَانَ مِنْ عِنْدِ اللهِ ثُمَّ كَفَرْتُمْ بِهٖ مَنْ اَضَلُّ مِمَّنْ هُوَ فِيْ شِقَاقٍۭ بَعِيْدٍ

57

IDGHAAM اِدْغَامُ

Idghaam means to pray the next mutaharrik letter after a noon saakin or tanween instead of the noon saakin or tanween.

2a) *idghaam* - There will be *idghaam* without *ghunna* when there is a ل or راء from the word يَرْمَلُوۡنَ after a *noon saakin* or *tanween*.

example: غَفُوۡرٌ رَّحِيۡمٌ and مِنۡ لَّدُنۡهُ

2b) There will be idghaam with ghunna when one of the letters يَاء و مر ن appear after a *noon saakin* or *tanween*.

example: مَنۡ يَّقُوۡلُ and رَسُوۡلًا مِّنۡهُمۡ

Note that in the 4 words بُنۡيَانٌ دُنۡيَا قِنۡوَانٌ صِنۡوَانٌ, there will be no *idghaam* because the *noon saakin* and the و or

يَاء after it are both in the same word. There will, however, be *izhaar (no ghunna)*.

This *izhaar* is called *izhaar mutlaq*.

EXERCISE

1.Underline all *idghaams* below. 2.Write *G* under each *ghunnah*.
3. Write *W* if it is without *ghunnah* 4. Read the verses

١. وَقَالُوا هٰذِهٖ اَنْعَامٌ وَّحَرْثٌ حِجْرٌ لَّا يَطْعَمُهَآ اِلَّا مَنْ نَّشَآءُ بِزَعْمِهِمْ

٢. قَالَ يٰقَوْمِ اَرَءَيْتُمْ اِنْ كُنْتُ عَلَىٰ بَيِّنَةٍ مِّنْ رَّبِّيْ

٣. فَقَدْ جَآءَكُمْ بَيِّنَةٌ مِّنْ رَّبِّكُمْ وَهُدًى وَّرَحْمَةٌ

٤. وَلَوْ تَوَاعَدْتُّمْ لَاخْتَلَفْتُمْ فِي الْمِيْعٰدِ وَلٰكِنْ لِّيَقْضِيَ اللّٰهُ اَمْرًا كَانَ مَفْعُوْلًا لِّيَهْلِكَ مَنْ هَلَكَ

٥. مَثَلُ الْجَنَّةِ الَّتِيْ وُعِدَ الْمُتَّقُوْنَ فِيْهَآ اَنْهَارٌ مِّنْ مَّآءٍ غَيْرِ اٰسِنٍ وَّاَنْهَارٌ مِّنْ لَّبَنٍ لَّمْ يَتَغَيَّرْ طَعْمُهٗ وَاَنْهَارٌ مِّنْ خَمْرٍ لَّذَّةٍ لِّلشَّارِبِيْنَ وَاَنْهَارٌ مِّنْ عَسَلٍ مُّصَفًّى

59

IQLAAB إِقْلَاب

3) *Iqlaab* happens when there is a ب after a ن saakin or

tanween. In iqlaab, the ن is spoken as a م.

examples: مِنۢ بَعْدُ and سَمِيعٌ ۢبَصِيرٌ:

EXERCISE

Underline all the *iqlaabs* below. Then read the verses.

١. اِذَا انۢبَعَثَ اَشْقَاهَا

٢. فَاَنۢبَتۡنَا فِيهَا حَبًّا

٣. فَكَانَتۡ هَبَآءً مُّنۢبَثًّا

٤. اِنَّ اللهَ سَمِيعٌ ۢبَصِيرٌ

٥. وَمَا يَنۢبَغِي لَهُمۡ وَمَا يَسۡتَطِيعُوۡنَ

٦. وَاَنۢبَتۡنَا عَلَيۡهِ شَجَرَةً مِّنۡ يَّقۡطِينٍ

60

اِخْفَاءُ IKHFAA

4)*Ikhfaa* happens when one of the remaining 15 letters (that is, the letters excluding the *idghaam*, *izhaar* and *iqlaab* letters)

comes after a ن saakin or tanween.

The 15 letters are:

$$\text{ت ث ج د ذ ز س ش ص ض ط ظ ف ق ك}$$

Examples: كُلَّا ضَرَبْنَا and اِنْ كُنْتُمْ

This *ikhfaa* is called *ikhfaa haqeeqi*.

EXERCISE

1. Underline the *ikhfaas* below 2. Read the verses.

١. لِكُلِّ امْرِئٍ مِّنْهُمْ يَوْمَئِذٍ شَأْنٌ يُّغْنِيْهِ

٢. قُلْ اِنِّيْ لَنْ يُّجِيْرَنِيْ مِنَ اللّٰهِ اَحَدٌ وَّلَنْ اَجِدَ مِنْ دُوْنِهِ

مُلْتَحَدًا

٣. وَاَنَّا مِنَّا الْمُسْلِمُوْنَ وَمِنَّا الْقَاسِطُوْنَ فَمَنْ اَسْلَمَ

فَأُولٰئِكَ تَحَرَّوْا رَشَدًا

61

٤. اِنَّ الَّذِيْنَ اٰمَنُوْا وَعَمِلُوا الصّٰلِحٰتِ لَهُمْ جَنّٰتٌ تَجْرِيْ مِنْ تَحْتِهَا الْاَنْهَارُ ذٰلِكَ الْفَوْزُ الْكَبِيْرُ

٥. اَمَّنْ هٰذَا الَّذِيْ هُوَ جُنْدٌ لَّكُمْ يَنْصُرُكُمْ مِّنْ دُوْنِ الرَّحْمٰنِ

٦. جَزَآؤُهُمْ عِنْدَ رَبِّهِمْ جَنّٰتُ عَدْنٍ تَجْرِيْ مِنْ تَحْتِهَا الْاَنْهٰرُ خٰلِدِيْنَ فِيْهَآ اَبَدًا

٧. قَالُوْا بَلٰى قَدْ جَآءَنَا نَذِيْرٌ فَكَذَّبْنَا وَقُلْنَا مَا نَزَّلَ اللّٰهُ مِنْ شَيْءٍ اِنْ اَنْتُمْ اِلَّا فِيْ ضَلَالٍ كَبِيْرٍ

٨. اِنَّآ اَرْسَلْنَا نُوْحًا اِلٰى قَوْمِهٖٓ اَنْ اَنْذِرْ قَوْمَكَ مِنْ قَبْلِ اَنْ يَّأْتِيَهُمْ عَذَابٌ اَلِيْمٌ

1.6.2: THE RULES OF MEEN SAAKIN مِيْمُ سَاكِنْ

A م *saakin* is a م with a *sukoon* on it.

Example: اَمُ

There are 3 rules for م *saakin*.
1) *idghaam*
2) *ikhfaa*
3) *izhaar*

IDGHAAM إِدْغَامُ

1) *idghaam* - when there is a م after a م *saakin*, then there will be *ghunnah* **and** *idghaam*.
This *idghaam* is called *idghaam sagheer mithlayn*.

Example: اَمُ مَّنْ

IKHFAA إِخْفَاءُ

2) *ikhfaa* happens when there is a ب after a م *saakin*.

Example: يَعْتَصِمُ بِاللّهِ.
This is called ikhfaa shafawii.

IZHAAR اِظْهَارْ

3) *Izhaar* - When any of the remaining 26 letters (any letter besides م and ب) appears after a م *saakin*, then *izhaar* will happen (no *ghunna*).

Example: اَلَمْ تَرَ

This is called *izhaar shafawii*

Note: You must read م *mushaddad* and ن *mushaddad* with *ghunna*. Both *Meem mushaddad* and *noon mushaddad* result in an *idghaam* with *ghunnah*.

Examples: اِنَّ اللّٰه ثُمَّ

EXERCISE

1. Underline each of the meem saakin and meem mushaddads below.
2. write D under it if it is idghaam
3. write K under it if it is Ikhfaa,
4. write Z under it if it is Izhaar.
5. Read the verses

١. يَغْفِرْ لَكُمْ مِّنْ ذُنُوْبِكُمْ وَيُؤَخِّرْكُمْ اِلٰٓى اَجَلٍ مُّسَمًّى

اِنَّ اَجَلَ اللّٰهِ اِذَا جَآءَ لَا يُؤَخَّرُ لَوْ كُنْتُمْ تَعْلَمُوْنَ

٢. اَمْ تَسْـَٔلُهُمْ اَجْرًا فَهُمْ مِّنْ مَّغْرَمٍ مُّثْقَلُوْنَ

٣. وَاِنِّيْ كُلَّمَا دَعَوْتُهُمْ لِتَغْفِرَ لَهُمْ جَعَلُوْۤا اَصَابِعَهُمْ فِيْۤ اٰذَانِهِمْ وَاسْتَغْشَوْا ثِيَابَهُمْ وَاَصَرُّوْا وَاسْتَكْبَرُوا اسْتِكْبَارًا

٤. مِمَّا خَطِيْٓـٰٔتِهِمْ اُغْرِقُوْا فَاُدْخِلُوْا نَارًا فَلَمْ يَجِدُوْا لَهُمْ مِّنْ دُوْنِ اللّٰهِ اَنْصَارًا

٥. وَيَطُوْفُ عَلَيْهِمْ وِلْدَانٌ مُّخَلَّدُوْنَ اِذَا رَاَيْتَهُمْ حَسِبْتَهُمْ لُؤْلُؤًا مَّنْثُوْرًا

بِسْمِ اللهِ الرَّحْمٰنِ الرَّحِيْم
وَرَتِّلِ الْقُرْاٰنَ تَرْتِيْلاً ۚ

Tajweed
for
Young Children

Part 2

1.7 - CHARACTERISTICS OF SOUNDS صِفَات

sifaat - pronouncing every letter clearly, as it should be pronounced, is called saying it with its *sifaat*.

There are 2 types of *sifaat*:
1) *sifaat laazima* (صِفَاتُ لَازِمَةٌ)
2) *sifaat aarida* (صِفَاتُ عَارِضَةٌ)

1) *sifaat laazima* - A *sifat laazima* is always there. If the letter is read without that characteristic, then the letter will not sound clear.
Failing to apply the *sifaat laazima* will result in *lahn jalii*.

2) *sifaat aarida* - A *sifat aarida* is not always there.
Failing to apply the *sifaat aarida* will result in *lahn khafii*.

THE CHAPTER ON THE SIFAAT LAAZIMA صِفَاتٌ لَازِمَةٌ

There are 17 *sifaat laazima*. The *sifaat laazima* are broken down into 2 groups:

i) *sifaat mutadhaada* (صِفَاتٌ مُتَضَادَّةٌ)

ii) *sifaat ghayr mutadhaada* (صِفَاتٌ غَيْرُ مُتَضَادَّةٌ)

i) A *sifaat mutadhaada* is one with an opposite.
i) A *sifaat ghayr mutadhaada* is one without an opposite.

TYPES OF SIFAAT MUTADHAADA صِفَاتٌ مُتَضَادَّةٌ

There are 10 *sifaat mutadhaada* (صِفَاتٌ مُتَضَادَّةٌ).
5 of the *sifaat* are opposites of the other 5. They are:

جَهْرٌ and هَمْسٌ

شِدَّتٌ and (تَوَسُّطٌ and) رِخْوَتٌ

اِسْتِعْلَاءٌ and اِسْتِفَالٌ

اِطْبَاقٌ and اِنْفِتَاحٌ

اِذْلَاقٌ and اِصْمَاتٌ

Note: the opposing *sifaat* should be read together as pairs.

Examples: *hams* and *jahr*,
              shiddat and *rikhwat*, etc.

SIFAT HAMS هَمْس

1a) *sifat hams* is a sound in which the voice softens and the breath remains constant.

Example: the س in مِسْكِين

There are 10 letters that have *sifat hams* in them. They can be remembered by remembering the phrase:

فَحَثَّهُ شَخْصٌ سَكَتْ

SIFAT JAHR جَهْر

1b) *sifat jahr* - This is the opposite of a *hams* sound. In *sifat jahr*, the voice rises and the breath pauses.

Example: the ء in يَأْتِي

The *sifaat jahr* letters are the other 19 letters that don't have *sifat hams*.

EXERCISE

1. Underline all the *sifat hams* in the verses below
2. Read them correctly

1. فَاعْتَرَفُوا بِذَنْبِهِمْ فَسُحْقًا لِّاَصْحٰبِ السَّعِيرِ

2. ثُمَّ فِي سِلْسِلَةٍ ذَرْعُهَا سَبْعُونَ ذِرَاعًا فَاسْلُكُوهُ

69

3. خِتْمُهُ مِسْكٌ وَّفِي ذٰلِكَ فَلْيَتَنَافَسِ الْمُتَنَافِسُوْنَ

4. فَسَبِّحْ بِحَمْدِ رَبِّكَ وَاسْتَغْفِرْهُ إِنَّهُ كَانَ تَوَّابًا

5. إِنَّ هٰذِهِ تَذْكِرَةٌ فَمَنْ شَآءَ اتَّخَذَ إِلٰى رَبِّهِ سَبِيْلًا

6. فَاصْبِرْ لِحُكْمِ رَبِّكَ وَلَا تُطِعْ مِنْهُمْ اٰثِمًا اَوْ كَفُوْرًا

7. بِسْمِ اللهِ الرَّحْمٰنِ الرَّحِيْمِ هَلْ اَتٰكَ حَدِيْثُ الْغَاشِيَةِ

8. وَجَعَلْنَا فِيْهَا رَوَاسِيَ شٰمِخٰتٍ وَّاَسْقَيْنٰكُمْ مَّآءً فُرَاتًا

9. يٰٓاَيُّهَا الْاِنْسَانُ اِنَّكَ كَادِحٌ اِلٰى رَبِّكَ كَدْحًا فَمُلٰقِيْهِ

SIFAT SHIDDAH شِدَّةُ

2a) *shiddah* - A *sifat shiddah* is one in which the voice stops forcefully.

Example: the **د** in اَحَدُ ٥ْ

There are 8 *shiddah* sounds. They are found in the phrase:

اَجِدُ قَطٍ بَكَتْ

SIFAT RIKHWAH رِخْوَةُ

2b) *rikhwah* - A *sifat rikhwah* is the opposite of a *sifat shiddah*. A *sifat rikhwah* causes the sound to continue and soften.

Example: the ش in بُشْرٰى

There are 16 *rikhwah* sounds. All sounds other than *shiddah* and *tawassut* sounds are *rikhwah* sounds.

SIFAT TAWASSUT تَوَسُّط

2c) Between the *sifat shiddah* and *sifat rikhwah* sounds, there is another category of *tawassut* sounds.

A *tawassut* sound is one that neither causes the voice to stop forcefully, nor does the sound continue smoothly. A *tawassut* sound is somewhere in between a *shiddah* and *rikhwah* sound.

Example: the ل in اَلَمْ يَجْعَلْ

The 5 *tawassut* letters are found in the words لِنْ عُمَرُ

EXERCISE

1. underline the *shiddah* letters and write S under them.
2. underline the *tawassut* letters and write T under them.
3. read all the verses.

١. وَمَا تَفَرَّقَ الَّذِيْنَ اُوْتُوا الْكِتَابَ اِلَّا مِنْۢ بَعْدِ مَا جَآءَتْهُمُ الْبَيِّنَةُ

٢. لِّيَعْلَمَ اَنْ قَدْ اَبْلَغُوْا رِسٰلٰتِ رَبِّهِمْ وَاَحَاطَ بِمَا لَدَيْهِمْ وَاَحْصٰى كُلَّ شَيْءٍ عَدَدًا

٣. اَلَّذِيْ خَلَقَ سَبْعَ سَمٰوٰتٍ طِبَاقًا مَّا تَرٰى فِيْ خَلْقِ الرَّحْمٰنِ مِنْ تَفٰوُتٍ فَارْجِعِ الْبَصَرَ هَلْ تَرٰى مِنْ فُطُوْرٍ

٤. جَزَآؤُهُمْ عِنْدَ رَبِّهِمْ جَنّٰتُ عَدْنٍ تَجْرِيْ مِنْ تَحْتِهَا الْاَنْهَارُ خَالِدِيْنَ فِيْهَآ اَبَدًا رَّضِيَ اللهُ عَنْهُمْ وَرَضُوْا عَنْهُ ذٰلِكَ لِمَنْ خَشِيَ رَبَّهٗ

72

SIFAT ISTI'LAA اِسْتِعْلَاء

3a) sifat *isti'laa* – A *sifat isti'laa* is one that causes the back tongue to rise and make contact with the roof of the mouth, causing the letter to become full mouthed and round-lipped.

Example: the ق in قَالَ

There are 7 *isti'laa* sounds. They are found in the words:

SIFAT ISTIFAAL اِسْتِفَالُ

3b) *Sifat istifaal* – A *sifat istifaal* is the opposite of *sifat isti'laa*. It causes the back tongue to stay low, and not rise up towards the roof of the mouth. As a result, the letters are empty mouthed.

Example: the س in سَلَاسِل

The 22 letters that are not *isti'laa* letters are *istifaal* letters.

EXERCISE

1. underline the *isti'laa* letters
2. read all the verses.

1. صِرَاطَ الَّذِيْنَ اَنْعَمْتَ عَلَيْهِمْ غَيْرِ الْمَغْضُوْبِ عَلَيْهِمْ وَلَا الضَّآلِّيْنَ

٢. وَاَنْ لَّوِ اسْتَقَامُوا عَلَى الطَّرِيقَةِ لَاَسْقَيْنٰهُمْ مَّآءً غَدَقًا

٣. اِلَّا الَّذِيْنَ اٰمَنُوْا وَعَمِلُوا الصّٰلِحٰتِ وَتَوَاصَوْا بِالْحَقِّ وَتَوَاصَوْا بِالصَّبْرِ

٤. الَّذِيْ خَلَقَ سَبْعَ سَمٰوٰتٍ طِبَاقًا مَا تَرٰى فِيْ خَلْقِ الرَّحْمٰنِ مِنْ تَفٰوُتٍ فَارْجِعِ الْبَصَرَ هَلْ تَرٰى مِنْ فُطُوْرٍ

٥. اَوَلَمْ يَرَوْا اِلَى الطَّيْرِ فَوْقَهُمْ صٰٓفّٰتٍ وَّيَقْبِضْنَ مَا يُمْسِكُهُنَّ اِلَّا الرَّحْمٰنُ اِنَّهٗ بِكُلِّ شَيْءٍ بَصِيْرٌ

٦. سَخَّرَهَا عَلَيْهِمْ سَبْعَ لَيَالٍ وَّثَمٰنِيَةَ اَيَّامٍ حُسُوْمًا فَتَرَى الْقَوْمَ فِيْهَا صَرْعٰى كَاَنَّهُمْ اَعْجَازُ نَخْلٍ خَاوِيَةٍ

SIFAT ITBAAQ اِطْبَاقْ

4a) *sifat itbaaq* – A *sifat itbaaq* is one which causes the middle tongue to rise and connect lightly with the roof of the mouth.

example: the ط ط in اَطْعَمَهُمْ

There are 4 *sifat itbaaq*. They are: ظ ط ض ص

SIFAT INFITAAH اِنْفِتَاحْ

4b) *sifat infitaah* – A *sifat infitah* is one which causes the middle tongue to stay low, and not move towards the roof.

Example: the ك ك in كَيْفَ

The 25 sounds that are not *sifat itbaaq* are *sifat infitah*.

EXERCISE

1. underline the *itbaaq* letters
2. read all the verses.

١. وَقَدْ اَضَلُّوْا كَثِيْرًا وَّلَا تَزِدِ الظّٰلِمِيْنَ اِلَّا ضَلَالًا

٢. صِرَاطَ الَّذِيْنَ اَنْعَمْتَ عَلَيْهِمْ غَيْرِ الْمَغْضُوْبِ عَلَيْهِمْ وَلَا الضَّآلِّيْنَ

75

3. اِلَّا الَّذِيْنَ اٰمَنُوْا وَعَمِلُوا الصّٰلِحٰتِ وَتَوَاصَوْا بِالْحَقِّ وَتَوَاصَوْا بِالصَّبْرِ

4. اِنَّا بَلَوْنٰهُمْ كَمَا بَلَوْنَآ اَصْحٰبَ الْجَنَّةِ اِذْ اَقْسَمُوْا لَيَصْرِمُنَّهَا مُصْبِحِيْنَ

5. عَلِيْهِمْ ثِيَابُ سُنْدُسٍ خُضْرٌ وَّاِسْتَبْرَقٌ وَّحُلُّوْٓا اَسَاوِرَ مِنْ فِضَّةٍ وَّسَقٰهُمْ رَبُّهُمْ شَرَابًا طَهُوْرًا

6. اَلَّذِيْ خَلَقَ سَبْعَ سَمٰوٰتٍ طِبَاقًا مَّا تَرٰى فِيْ خَلْقِ الرَّحْمٰنِ مِنْ تَفٰوُتٍ فَارْجِعِ الْبَصَرَ هَلْ تَرٰى مِنْ فُطُوْرٍ

7. اَوَلَمْ يَرَوْا اِلَى الطَّيْرِ فَوْقَهُمْ صٰٓفّٰتٍ وَّيَقْبِضْنَ مَا يُمْسِكُهُنَّ اِلَّا الرَّحْمٰنُ اِنَّهٗ بِكُلِّ شَيْءٍۢ بَصِيْرٌ

76

SIFAT IZLAAQ اِذْلَاقْ

5a) sifat izlaaq – a sifat izlaaq makes a letter smooth with the help of the tongue and lips.

Example: the ف in فَآئِرُوْنَ

There are 6 sifat izlaaq letters. They are found in the words:

فَرَّ مِنْ لُبٍّ

SIFAT ISMAAT اِصْمَاتْ

5b) sifat ismaat – a sifat ismaat is the opposite of a sifat izlaaq. It is pronounced with some pressure.

Example: the س in سلاسل.

The 23 sounds that are not sifat izlaaq are sifat ismaat.

EXERCISE

1. underline the izlaaq letters
2. read all the verses.

١. اَمَّنْ هٰذَا الَّذِيْ هُوَ جُنْدٌ لَّكُمْ يَنْصُرُكُمْ مِّنْ دُوْنِ الرَّحْمٰنِ اِنِ الْكَافِرُوْنَ اِلَّا فِيْ غُرُوْرٍ

77

٢. قُلْ اُوحِيَ اِلَيَّ اَنَّهُ اسْتَمَعَ نَفَرٌ مِنَ الْجِنِّ فَقَالُوٓا اِنَّا سَمِعْنَا قُرْاٰنًا عَجَبًا

٣. اِنَّاۤ اَرْسَلْنَا نُوحًا اِلٰى قَوْمِهٖۤ اَنْ اَنْذِرْ قَوْمَكَ مِنْ قَبْلِ اَنْ يَّاْتِيَهُمْ عَذَابٌ اَلِيْمٌ

٤. رَبِّ اغْفِرْ لِيْ وَلِوَالِدَيَّ وَلِمَنْ دَخَلَ بَيْتِيَ مُؤْمِنًا وَّلِلْمُؤْمِنِيْنَ وَالْمُؤْمِنٰتِ وَلَا تَزِدِ الظّٰلِمِيْنَ اِلَّا تَبَارًا

٥. لَمْ يَكُنِ الَّذِيْنَ كَفَرُوْا مِنْ اَهْلِ الْكِتٰبِ وَالْمُشْرِكِيْنَ مُنْفَكِّيْنَ حَتّٰى تَاْتِيَهُمُ الْبَيِّنَةُ

٦. جَزَآؤُهُمْ عِنْدَ رَبِّهِمْ جَنّٰتُ عَدْنٍ تَجْرِيْ مِنْ تَحْتِهَا الْاَنْهَارُ خٰلِدِيْنَ فِيْهَاۤ اَبَدًا رَضِيَ اللهُ عَنْهُمْ وَرَضُوْا عَنْهُ ذٰلِكَ لِمَنْ خَشِيَ رَبَّهٗ

1.8 – SIFAAT GHAYR MUTADHAADA غَيْرُ مُتَضَادَّةٌ

There are 7 types of *ghayr mutadhaada* letters.
They are:

1. صَفِيْرُ

2. قَلْقَلَةُ

3. لِيْنُ

4. اِنْحِرَافُ

5. تَكْرِيْرُ

6. تَفَشِّيْ

7. اِسْتِطَالَةُ

SIFAT SAFEER صَفِيْرُ

1) A *safeer* letter comes out forcefully, and has a slight whistle too.

Example: the س in وَالسَّمَاءِ

There are 3 *safeer* letters. They are: ز س ص

EXERCISE

1. underline the *safeer* letters;   2. read all the verses.

١. عٰلِيَهُمْ ثِيَابُ سُنْدُسٍ خُضْرٌ وَّاِسْتَبْرَقٌ وَّحُلُّوٓا اَسَاوِرَ مِنْ فِضَّةٍ وَّسَقٰهُمْ رَبُّهُمْ شَرَابًا طَهُوْرًا

٢. سَخَّرَهَا عَلَيْهِمْ سَبْعَ لَيَالٍ وَّثَمٰنِيَةَ اَيَّامٍ حُسُوْمًا فَتَرَى الْقَوْمَ فِيْهَا صَرْعٰى كَاَنَّهُمْ اَعْجَازُ نَخْلٍ خَاوِيَةٍ

٣. وَاِنِّيْ كُلَّمَا دَعَوْتُهُمْ لِتَغْفِرَ لَهُمْ جَعَلُوٓا اَصَابِعَهُمْ فِيْٓ اٰذَانِهِمْ وَاسْتَغْشَوْا ثِيَابَهُمْ وَاَصَرُّوْا وَاسْتَكْبَرُوا اسْتِكْبَارًا

80

SIFAT QALQALA قَلْقَلَةٌ

2) A *qalqala* letter is one which echoes all around the mouth and is quite strong. *Qalqala* normally happens if the letter is *saakin* or *waqf* (a letter you stopped reading on).

Example: the ق in خَلَقَ and خَلَقْتَ

There are 5 *qalqala* letters. They are found in the words:

قُطْبُ جَدٍّ

EXERCISE

1. underline the *qalqala* letters ;   2. read all the verses.

ثُمَّ خَلَقْنَا النُّطْفَةَ عَلَقَةً فَخَلَقْنَا الْعَلَقَةَ مُضْغَةً فَخَلَقْنَا

الْمُضْغَةَ عِظَامًا فَكَسَوْنَا الْعِظَامَ لَحْمًا قُلِ ادْعُوا اللّٰهَ اَوِ

ادْعُوا الرَّحْمٰنَ اَيًّا مَّا تَدْعُوْا فَلَهُ الْاَسْمَآءُ الْحُسْنٰى ٥ اَلَّذِيْنَ

اٰمَنُوْا وَتَطْمَئِنُّ قُلُوْبُهُمْ بِذِكْرِ اللّٰهِ اَلَا بِذِكْرِ اللّٰهِ تَطْمَئِنُّ

الْقُلُوْبُ ٥ حَتّٰى اِذَا بَلَغَ مَطْلِعَ الشَّمْسِ وَجَدَهَا تَطْلُعُ عَلٰى

قَوْمٍ لَّمْ نَجْعَلْ لَّهُمْ مِّنْ دُوْنِهَا سِتْرًا٥ وَلَا تَطْرُدِ الَّذِيْنَ

يَدْعُوْنَ رَبَّهُمْ بِالْغَدَاةِ وَالْعَشِيِّ يُرِيْدُوْنَ وَجْهَهُ ٥وَاِنْ

كَانُوْا مِنْ قَبْلِ اَنْ يُّنَزَّلَ عَلَيْهِمْ مِّنْ قَبْلِهِ لَمُبْلِسِيْنَ٥

81

SIFAT LEEN لِين

3) A *leen* letter is one that is so soft that it can be read as a *madd* - in other words, it can be stretched.

Examples: بَيْتٍ and مَوْتٍ

Leen occurs when a واو or يَاء has a *sukoon*, and there is a letter with a *zabar* before it.

EXERCISE

1. underline the *leen* letters ;   2. read all the verses.

١. قَالَ رَبِّ اِنِّيْ دَعَوْتُ قَوْمِيْ لَيْلًا وَّنَهَارًا

٢. وَوُجُوْهٌ يَّوْمَئِذٍ عَلَيْهَا غَبَرَةٌ

٣. وَالْمَلَكُ عَلَى اَرْجَآئِهَا وَيَحْمِلُ عَرْشَ رَبِّكَ فَوْقَهُمْ يَوْمَئِذٍ ثَمَانِيَةٌ

٤. اِلَّا الَّذِيْنَ اٰمَنُوْا وَعَمِلُوا الصّٰلِحٰتِ وَتَوَاصَوْا بِالْحَقِّ وَتَوَاصَوْا بِالصَّبْرِ

SIFAT INHIRAAF اِنْحِرَاف

4) *Inhiraaf* causes the sound of the letter ل to focus at the end of the tongue, and that of the letter رَاء to focus a little further back.

Example: يَآ اَيُّهَا الرَّسُوْلُ should be read so that the ل and رَاء sound clearly different.

There are 2 *inhiraaf* letters. They are لَام and رَاء.

SIFAT TAKREER تَكْرِيْر

5) *Takreer* stops the sound of a letter staying in one place. A *Takreer* letter should be read in such a way that the رَاء neither appears to have doubled, nor does it sound like a وَاو.

Example: the رَاء in اَلرَّحْمٰنِ الرَّحِيْمِ ۖ

Takreer is found only in the letter رَاء.

EXERCISE

1. underline the *inhiraaf* and *takreer* letters
2. read all the verses.

١. الَّذِي خَلَقَ سَبْعَ سَمٰوٰتٍ طِبَاقًا مَّا تَرٰى فِي خَلْقِ الرَّحْمٰنِ مِنْ تَفٰوُتٍ فَارْجِعِ الْبَصَرَ هَلْ تَرٰى مِنْ فُطُوْرٍ

٢. اِلَّا بَلٰغًا مِّنَ اللهِ وَرِسٰلٰتِهٖ وَمَنْ يَّعْصِ اللهَ وَرَسُوْلَهٗ فَاِنَّ لَهٗ نَارَ جَهَنَّمَ خَالِدِيْنَ فِيْهَا أَبَدًا

٣. اِنَّ الَّذِيْنَ كَفَرُوْا مِنْ اَهْلِ الْكِتٰبِ وَالْمُشْرِكِيْنَ فِيْ نَارِ جَهَنَّمَ خٰلِدِيْنَ فِيْهَا أُولٰٓئِكَ هُمْ شَرُّ الْبَرِيَّةِ

٤. يَغْفِرْ لَكُمْ مِّنْ ذُنُوْبِكُمْ وَيُؤَخِّرْكُمْ اِلٰٓى اَجَلٍ مُّسَمًّى اِنَّ اَجَلَ اللهِ اِذَا جَآءَ لَا يُؤَخَّرُ لَوْ كُنْتُمْ تَعْلَمُوْنَ

SIFAT TAFASH-SHII تَفَشِّي

6) *Sifat tafash-shii* causes the sound to fill the entire mouth.

Example: the ش in شَآءَ

Tafash-shii happens only in the letter ش.

EXERCISE

1. underline the *tafashii* letters
2. read all the verses.

١. ثُمَّ شَقَقْنَا الْاَرْضَ شَقًّا

٢. فَمَا تَنْفَعُهُمْ شَفَاعَةُ الشَّافِعِينَ

٣. وَمَا تَشَآءُوْنَ اِلَّا اَنْ يَّشَآءَ اللّٰهُ رَبُّ الْعَلَمِينَ

٤. اِنَّ نَاشِئَةَ الَّيْلِ هِيَ اَشَدُّ وَطْئًا وَّاَقْوَمُ قِيْلًا

٥. اَمْ لَهُمْ شُرَكَآءُ فَلْيَأْتُوْا بِشُرَكَآىِٕهِمْ اِنْ كَانُوْا صٰدِقِينَ

٦. يَهْدِيْ اِلَى الرُّشْدِ فَاٰمَنَّا بِهٖ وَلَنْ نُّشْرِكَ بِرَبِّنَآ اَحَدًا

85

ISTITAALA اِسْتِطَالَةُ

Istitaala causes a sound to continue from the same place, with no variation at all.

Example: the ض in وَلَا الضَّآلِّينَ ۚ.

Istitaala happens only in the letter ض.

The ضا should not sound like a د or ظا.

EXERCISE

1. underline the *istitaala* letters
2. read all the verses.

١. وَكُنَّا نَخُوضُ مَعَ الْخَآئِضِينَ

٢. اِرْجِعِيٓ اِلٰى رَبِّكِ رَاضِيَةً مَّرْضِيَّةً

٣. فَاَقْبَلَ بَعْضُهُمْ عَلٰى بَعْضٍ يَّتَلَاوَمُوْنَ

٤. صِرَاطَ الَّذِيْنَ اَنْعَمْتَ عَلَيْهِمْ غَيْرِ الْمَغْضُوْبِ عَلَيْهِمْ وَلَا الضَّآلِّينَ

1.9 – MADD مَدّ

1.9.1: WHAT IS MADD?

Stretching the sound of a *harf madd* or *harf leen* is called *madd*.

WHAT IS A HARF MADD مَدّ?

الف, واو and يَاء are the *harf madd*. *Madd* can only be stretched if one of these letters is present.

Examples: نُوحِيْهَا

WHAT IS A HARF LEEN لِيْن

When there is a *zabar* before واو *saakin* or يَاء *saakin*, it is called *harf leen*.

Examples: والصَّيْفِ   مِنْ خَوْفٍ

WHAT IS TUWL طُوْل?

Tuwl is stretching a letter for 3-5 *alifs*.

WHAT IS TAWASSUT تَوَسُّط?

Tawassut is stretching a letter for 2-3 *alifs*.

WHAT IS QASR قَصْر?

Qasr is stretching a letter for 1 *alif*.

1.9.2 : TYPES OF MADD مَدّ

There are 2 types of *madd*. They are:

1) *Madd asli* اَصْلِيّ

2) *Madd far'ee* فَرْعِيّ

WHAT IS MADD ASLI اَصْلِيّ?

If there isn't a ء (hamzah) or *sukoon(jazm)* immediately after the *harf madd*, then the *madd* is called *madd asli*.

Example: نُوْحِيْهَا

Qasr is necessary in this.

EXERCISE

1. Underline all the *madd asli* in this passage
2. read the passage.

Note: Remember that a letter with a vertical zabar, vertical zer or upside-down pesh is also a *madd asli*:

WHAT IS MADD FAR'EE فَرْعِيّ؟

If there is a ء (hamzah) or sukoon (jazm) immediately after the harf madd, then the madd is called madd far'ee.

madd far'ee has the following types:

MADD MUTTASIL WAJIB مُتَّصِلٌ وَاجِبٌ

When a ء (hamzah) comes after a harf madd, and both are in the same word, it is madd muttasil wajib.

Examples: سَاءَ سُوٓءَ سِيٓءَ

Tuwl is necessary in such a madd.

MADD MUNFASIL WAJIB مُنْفَصِلٌ وَاجِبٌ

When a ء comes after a harf madd, and both are in different words, it is madd munfasil wajib.

Examples: الَّذِيٓ اَطْعَمَهُمْ   قَالُوٓا اٰمَنَّا   مَآ اَنْتَ

Both tuwl and tawassut are allowed in this madd.

EXERCISE

1. Underline the madds in the verses on the next page.
2. write t under it if it is a madd muttasil wajib
3. write n under it if is is a madd munfasil wajib
4. read the verses.

89

١. وَحَاجَّهٗ قَوْمُهٗ قَالَ اَتُحَاجُّوْٓنِّيْ فِي اللهِ وَقَدْ هَدَانِ وَلَاۤ اَخَافُ مَا تُشْرِكُوْنَ بِهٖۤ اِلَّاۤ اَنْ يَّشَاۤءَ رَبِّيْ شَيْـًٔا وَسِعَ رَبِّيْ كُلَّ شَيْءٍ عِلْمًا اَفَلَا تَتَذَكَّرُوْنَ

٢. اِنْ هِيَ اِلَّاۤ اَسْمَاۤءٌ سَمَّيْتُمُوْهَاۤ اَنْتُمْ وَاٰبَاۤؤُكُمْ مَّاۤ اَنْزَلَ اللهُ بِهَا مِنْ سُلْطَانٍ اِنْ يَّتَّبِعُوْنَ اِلَّا الظَّنَّ وَمَا تَهْوَى الْاَنْفُسُ وَلَقَدْ جَاۤءَهُمْ مِّنْ رَّبِّهِمُ الْهُدٰى

٣. وَجَوَزْنَا بِبَنِيْٓ اِسْرَاۤءِيْلَ الْبَحْرَ فَاَتْبَعَهُمْ فِرْعَوْنُ وَجُنُوْدُهٗ بَغْيًا وَّعَدْوًا حَتّٰى اِذَاۤ اَدْرَكَهُ الْغَرَقُ قَالَ اٰمَنْتُ اَنَّهٗ لَاۤ اِلٰهَ اِلَّا الَّذِيْٓ اٰمَنَتْ بِهٖ بَنُوْٓا اِسْرَاۤءِيْلَ وَاَنَا مِنَ الْمُسْلِمِيْنَ

MADD AARIDHI WAQFI عَارِضِيّ وَقْفِي

When a *sukoon asli* (an actual *sukoon*) is not present after a *harf madd*, but instead a *sukoon aaridhi* is present because of *waqf* (a *sukoon* that replaces a *harkat*), then *madd aaridhi waqfi* occurs there.

Example: خَالِدُوْنْ ← خَالِدُوْنَ

Tuwl, *tawassut* and *qasr* are all allowed in this *madd*.

MADD AARIDHI LEEN عَارِضِيّ لِيْن

madd aaridhi leen occurs when a *harf leen* is followed by a letter that has become *saakin* because of *waqf*.

Examples: بَيْتْ مَوْتْ ← بَيْتٍ مَوْتِ

Tuwl, *tawassut* and *qasr* are allowed in this *madd*, but *qasr* is preferred.

EXERCISE

1. underline all *madd aridh*. 2. Write W for *waqfi*, and L for *leen*.

بِسْمِ اللهِ الرَّحْمٰنِ الرَّحِيْمِ ٥ لِاِيْلَافِ قُرَيْشٍ ٥ وَاٰمَنَهُمْ

مِّنْ خَوْفٍ ٥ اَلَمْ نَجْعَلْ لَّهُ عَيْنَيْنِ ٥ بِاَيِّكُمُ الْمَفْتُوْنُ ٥

ثُمَّ الْجَحِيْمَ صَلُّوْهُ ٥ فَلْيَعْبُدُوْا رَبَّ هٰذَا الْبَيْتِ ٥ فَوَيْلٌ

لِّلْمُصَلِّيْنَ ٥ وَلِسَانًا وَّشَفَتَيْنِ ٥ وَمِزَاجُهُ مِنْ تَسْنِيْمٍ ٥

91

MADD LAAZIM WAJIB لَازِمٌ وَاجِبٌ

madd laazim wajib occurs when a *mushaddad* letter or *sukoon asli* appears after a *harf madd*.

Examples: وَلَا الضَّآلِّيْنَ ۝ اٰلْـٰٔنَ

Tuwl is necessary in this *madd*.

madd laazim wajib has a further 4 types:
1. Madd laazim kalmi muthaqqal
2. Madd laazim kalmi mukhaffaf
3. Madd laazim harfi muthaqqal
4. Madd laazim harfi mukhaffaf

1.9.3: TYPES OF MADD LAAZIM

MADD LAAZIM KALMI MUTHAQQAL كَلِمِيّ مُثَقَّلٌ

When a word has a *mushaddad* letter after a *harf madd*, then a *madd laazim kalmi muthaqqal* occurs.

Example: دَآبَّةٌ ۝

Tuwl must be done for such *madds*.

Note 1: it is called *kalmi* because the *harf madd* and the letter after it are in the **same** word.

Note 2: it is called *muthaqqal* because the letter after the *harf madd* is *mushaddad*.

92

MADD LAAZIM KALMI MUKHAFFAF كَلِمِيّ مُخَفَّفٌ

When a word has a *sukoon asli* after a *harf madd* then a *madd laazim kalmi mukhaffaf* occurs.

Example: ءَآلْئَٰنَ

Tuwl must be done for such *madds*.

Note 1: it is called *kalmi* because the *harf madd* and the letter after it are in the **same** word.

Note 2: it is called *mukhaffaf* because the letter after the *harf madd* is *saakin*.

EXERCISE

1. underline *madds* & Write Q for *muthaqqal*, & K for *mukhaffaf*.

مُدْهَآمَّتٰنِ ○ مَا الْحَآقَّةُ ○ وَوَجَدَكَ ضَآلًّا فَهَدٰى ○ فَاِذَا

جَآءَتِ الصَّآخَّةُ ○ وَاِنَّا لَنَحْنُ الصَّآفُّونَ ○ وَمَآ اَدْرٰىكَ مَا

الْحَآقَّةُ ○ فَاِذَا جَآءَتِ الطَّآمَّةُ الْكُبْرٰى ○ اَثُمَّ اِذَا مَا وَقَعَ

اٰمَنْتُمْ بِهٖ آلْئَٰنَ وَقَدْ كُنْتُمْ بِهٖ تَسْتَعْجِلُونَ ○ وَقَدْ

عَصَيْتَ قَبْلُ وَكُنْتَ مِنَ الْمُفْسِدِينَ ○ وَخَلَقَ الْجَآنَّ مِنْ

مَّارِجٍ مِّنْ نَّارٍ ○ اِنَّهُمْ اَلْفَوْا اٰبَآءَهُمْ ضَآلِّينَ ○

93

HUROOF MUQATTA'AAT مُقَطَّعَاتُ

Some surahs of the Holy Quran start with a series of letters that are read separately. They are called *huroof muqatta'aat*.

Examples: يٰسٓ قٓ صٓ

MADD LAAZIM HARFI MUTHAQQAL حَرْفِيّ مُثَقَّلُ

When a word has a *mushaddad* letter after a *harf madd* in a *harf muqatta'aat* then *madd laazim harfi muthaqqal* occurs.

Example: طٰسٓمّ

Tuwl must be done for such *madds*.

MADD LAAZIM HARFI MUKHAFFAF حَرْفِيّ مُخَفَّفُ

When a word has a *sukoon asli* after a *harf madd* in a *harf muqatta'aat* then a *Madd laazim kalmi mukhaffaf* occurs.

Example: صٓ قٓ

Tuwl must be done for such *madds*.

Note: *harfi muthaqqal* and *harfi mukhaffaf* only occur in *huroof muqatta'aat*.

EXERCISE – READ THE VERSES BELOW

طٰسٓمّ	طٰهٰ	كٓهيٰعٓصٓ	الٓمٓرٰ	الٓمٓصٓ	الٓمٓ
نٓ	قٓ	حٰمٓ عٓسٓقٓ	حٰمٓ	صٓ	يٰسٓ طٰسٓ

1.10 – WAQF وَقْفْ

WHAT IS WAQF وَقْفْ?

Taking a new breath by stopping at the end of a word is called *waqf*.

There are 3 types of *waqf*:

1. *Waqf bil iskaan*   2. *Waqf bir rawm*   3. *Waqf bil ishmaam*

WAQF BIL ISKAAN إِسْكَانْ

Making a *mutaharrik* letter into a *saakin* letter during waqf is called *waqf bil iskaan*.

Example: يَعْلَمُوْنَ ◄ يَعْلَمُوْنْ

EXERCISE – READ THE VERSES BELOW

وَلَا يَسْتَثْنُوْنَ۞ الرَّحْمٰنِ الرَّحِيْمِ۞ مٰلِكِ يَوْمِ الدِّيْنِ۞

فَتَنَادَوْا مُصْبِحِيْنَ۞ بَلْ نَحْنُ مَحْرُوْمُوْنَ۞ بِأَيِّكُمُ

الْمَفْتُوْنُ۞ فَأَصْبَحَتْ كَالصَّرِيْمِ۞ هَمَّازٍ مَّشَّاءٍ بِنَمِيْمٍ۞

فَسَتُبْصِرُ وَيُبْصِرُوْنَ۞ فَلَا تُطِعِ الْمُكَذِّبِيْنَ۞ عُتُلٍّ بَعْدَ

ذٰلِكَ زَنِيْمٍ۞ أَنْ كَانَ ذَا مَالٍ وَّبَنِيْنَ۞

95

WAQF BIR RAWM رَوْم

Pronouncing a *zer* or *pesh* or double *zer* or double *pesh* at the end of a word with only 1/3rd of the *harkat* is called *waqf bir rawm*.

Examples: نَسْتَعِيْنُ ۛ لَفِيْ خُسْرٍ ۛ

EXERCISE

1. underline all the *waqf bir rowm* in verses below.
2. read the verses, applying *waqf bir rowm* where it is present
3. apply *waqf bil iskaan* if *rowm* is not present.

بِسْمِ اللهِ الرَّحْمٰنِ الرَّحِيْمِ۝ مٰلِكِ يَوْمِ الدِّيْنِ۝

فَأَصْبَحَتْ كَالصَّرِيْمِ۝ وَلَا يَسْتَثْنُوْنَ۝ الرَّحْمٰنِ

الرَّحِيْمِ۝ فَتَنَادَوْا مُصْبِحِيْنَ۝ بَلْ نَحْنُ مَحْرُوْمُوْنَ۝

بِأَيِّكُمُ الْمَفْتُوْنُ۝ فَأَصْبَحَتْ كَالصَّرِيْمِ۝ فَسَتُبْصِرُ

وَيُبْصِرُوْنَ۝ فَلَا تُطِعِ الْمُكَذِّبِيْنَ۝ هَمَّازٍ مَّشَّاءٍ بِنَمِيْمٍ۝

عُتُلٍّ بَعْدَ ذٰلِكَ زَنِيْمٍ۝ أَنْ كَانَ ذَا مَالٍ وَّبَنِيْنَ۝

96

WAQF BIL ISHMAAM اِشْمَامْ

During *waqf,* making a *pesh* or 2 *pesh* at the end of a word into a *saakin* and at the same time, making an O shape with the lips,indicating a *pesh* is called *waqf bil ishmaam.*

Example: نَسْتَعِيْنُ ۖ

EXERCISE

1. underline all the *waqf bil ishmaam* in verses below.
2. read the verses, applying *waqf bil ishmaam* where present
3. apply *waqf bil iskaan* if *ishmaam* is not present.

فَكُّ رَقَبَةٍ۠ مَا الْحَآقَّةُ۠ نَارٌ حَامِيَةٌ۠ مَلِكِ النَّاسِ۠ اِلٰهِ

النَّاسِ۠ كِرَامٌ بَرَرَةٍ۠ لِيَوْمٍ عَظِيْمٍ۠ وَلَيَالٍ عَشْرٍ۠

وَطُوْرِ سِيْنِيْنَ۠ مَا الْقَارِعَةُ۠ كَلَّا لَا وَزَرَ۠ اَللّٰهُ الصَّمَدُ۠

خُذُوْهُ فَغُلُّوْهُ سَاُصْلِيْهِ سَقَرَ۠ كَلَّا وَالْقَمَرِ۠ وَخَسَفَ

الْقَمَرُ۠ وَقِيْلَ مَنْ رَاقٍ۠ لِيَوْمِ الْفَصْلِ۠ بِأَيْدِيْ سَفَرَةٍ۠

كِتَابٌ مَّرْقُوْمٌ۠

NOTES

Note 1: when a double *zabar* appears at the end of a word during *waqf*, the double *zabar* becomes single.

Example: اَفْوَاجًاؕ ← اَفْوَاجًا

EXERCISE

1. underline all the double zabars in the verses below.
2. read the verses, making the double zabars in to singles.
3. If the verse doesn't end in double zabar, apply *waqf bil iskan*.

سَاُرْهِقُهٗ صَعُوْدًاo ثُمَّ عَبَسَ وَبَسَرَo وَجَنّٰتٍ اَلْفَافًاo

حَدَآئِقَ وَاَعْنَابًاo وَكَوَاعِبَ اَتْرَابًاo وَّزَيْتُوْنًا وَّنَخْلًاo

مُّطَاعٍ ثَمَّ اَمِيْنٍo وَمَا هُوَ بِالْهَزْلِo وَوَالِدٍ وَّمَا وَلَدَo

لَتَرَوُنَّ الْجَحِيْمَo مٰلِكِ يَوْمِ الدِّيْنِo وَصَاحِبَتِهٖ

وَاَخِيْهِo فَقُتِلَ كَيْفَ قَدَّرَo فَالْعٰصِفٰتِ عَصْفًاo

وَالنّٰشِرَاتِ نَشْرًاo فَالْفٰرِقٰتِ فَرْقًاo اِلٰى قَدَرٍ مَّعْلُوْمٍo

وَالْجِبَالَ اَوْتَادًاo وَالنّٰشِطٰتِ نَشْطًاo

98

Note 2: when a round taa (ة) appears at the end of a word

during waqf, it becomes a haa (ه).

Example: جَنَّةٍ ○ ➔ جَنَّهْ

EXERCISE

1. underline all the round *taas* in verses below.
2. read the verses, making the round *taas* in to *haas*.

فَكُّ رَقَبَةٍ ○ مَا الْحَآقَّةُ ○ نَارٌ حَامِيَةٌ ○ مَلِكِ النَّاسِ ○ اِلٰهِ

النَّاسِ ○ جَزَآءً وِّفَاقًا ○ كِرَامٍ بَرَرَةٍ ○ لِيَوْمٍ عَظِيمٍ ○

وَلَيَالٍ عَشْرٍ ○ وَطُوْرِ سِيْنِيْنَ ○ مَا الْقَارِعَةُ ○ بِأَيْدِيْ

سَفَرَةٍ ○ كِتَابٌ مَّرْقُوْمٌ ○ كِرَامًا كَاتِبِيْنَ ○ فَأُمُّهُ هَاوِيَةٌ ○

قُطُوْفُهَا دَانِيَةٌ ○ اِلَّا الْمُصَلِّيْنَ ○ وَفَاكِهَةً وَّاَبًّا ○ تَرْهَقُهَا

قَتَرَةٌ ○ فَأَيْنَ تَذْهَبُوْنَ ○ اَلنَّجْمُ الثَّاقِبُ ○ عَامِلَةٌ

نَّاصِبَةٌ ○ فَلْيَدْعُ نَادِيَهْ ○ فِيْ جَنَّةٍ عَالِيَةٍ ○

SAKTAH سَكْتَةٌ

Pausing the sound for a moment – but not breaking the breath – is called *saktah*. In the Quran, it must be done in 4 places:

1. surah Kahf	وَلَمْ يَجْعَلْ لَّهُ عِوَجَا سكتة قَيِّمًا
2. surah Yaseen	مِنْ مَّرْقَدِنَا سكتة هٰذَا
3. surah Qiyamah	وَقِيلَ مَنْ سكتة رَاقٍ
4. surah Tatfeef	كَلَّا بَلْ سكتة رَانَ

تَمَّتْ بِالْخَيْرِ

رَبَّنَا تَقَبَّلْ مِنَّا إِنَّكَ أَنْتَ السَّمِيعُ الْعَلِيمُ ۙ

وَتُبْ عَلَيْنَا إِنَّكَ أَنْتَ التَّوَّابُ الرَّحِيمُ ۙ

وَأٰخِرُ دَعْوَانَا أَنِ الْحَمْدُ لِلّٰهِ رَبِّ الْعٰلَمِينَ ۙ

1.11 – Examples of putting tajweed into practice

HARF HAAFII - ض

To make this sound, the side of the tongue touches the gums of the teeth that are at the back of the mouth and on the left.

This is a full mouth letter.

Its *sifaat laazima mutadhadda* are:

1) Jahr
2) Rikhwah
3) Isti'laa
4) Itbaaq
5) Ismaat

Its *Sifaat ghayr mutadhaadda* are:

1) Istitaalat

HARF LAHWII - ك

To make this sound, the back of the tongue goes towards

the uvula, but further forward than ق, and touches the soft
palate.

This is an empty mouth letter.

Its *Sifaat laazima mutadhadda* are:
1) *hams*
2) *shiddah*
3) *istifaal*
4) *infitaah*
5) *Ismaat*

It has no *Sifaat ghayr mutadaadda*

1.12 - TRANSLATION OF IMPORTANT KEY TERMS

LESSON 1

Ta'awwuz:	Praying *a'uzubillah* – it means to seek refuge	تَعَوُّذ
Tasmiyyah:	Praying *bismillah* – it means to start	تَسْمِيَّة

LESSON 2

Tajweed	To create beauty – to pray the Quran correctly	تَجْوِيد
Lahn	Mistake (in other words, a *tajweed* mistake)	لَحْن
Jalii	A big, really obvious mistake	جَلِيّ
Khafii	A smaller, less obvious mistake. Only people who know *tajweed* will spot such mistakes	خَفِيّ
Saakin	A letter with a *jazm / sukoon* or it.	سَاكِن
Mutaharrik	A letter with a *zabar, zer* or *pesh* on it	مُتَحَرِّك
Isti'aalii	With a mouth full of air	إِسْتِعْلَائِيّ
Istifaalii	With a mouth empty of air	إِسْتِفَالِيّ
Izhaar	To make something obvious	إِظْهَار
Ikhfaa	To hide something	إِخْفَاء
Haraam	Not allowed – goes against shariah rules	حَرَام
Makrooh	Disliked or inappropriate	مَكْرُوه

LESSON 3

Makhraj	The starting point of a letter	مَخْرَجٌ
Makhaarij	The plural of *makhraj*	مَخَارِجُ
Madd	To stretch, pull or extend	مَدّ
Halq	Throat	حَلْقٌ
Halqi	Throat letters	حَلْقِيّ
Lahaat	Uvula	لَهَاةٌ
Lahawii	Letters that start from near the uvula	لَهَوِيّ
Shajara	Tree	شَجَرَةٌ
Shajarii	The roof of the mouth, which has branches like the branches of a tree	شَجَرِيّ
Haafa	Rear edge	حَافَةٌ
Haafii	Letters that are made with the rear edges of the tongue	حَافِيّ
Taraf	Front edge	طَرَف
Tarafii	Letters that are made with the front edges of the tongue	طَرَفِيّ
Nit'	tip	نِطْعُ
Nit'ee	Letters that are made with the tongue tip touching the hard palate	نِطْعِيّ
Thanaaya	The 4 big teeth that are furthest forward in the mouth	ثَنَايَا

104

Safeer	Whistle – like the tweeting of small birds	صَفِيْرُ
Shafa	Lips	شَفَةٌ
Shafawii	Lip letters	شَفَوِيّ
Ghunna	A humming sound, from the nose	غُنَّةٌ

LESSON 5

Isti'laaii	With a mouth full of air	اِسْتِعْلَائِيّ
istifaalii	With a mouth empty of air	اِسْتِفَالِيّ
Mushtarak	Mixed letters – letters that are sometimes prayed with a mouth full of air and sometimes with a mouth empty of air	مُشْتَرَكُ
Waqf	To stop	وَقْفُ

LESSON 6

Izhaar	To make something obvious and clear	اِظْهَارُ
Idghaam	To join or merge	اِدْغَامُ
Iqlaab	To change or replace	اِقْلَابُ
Mithlayn	2 same or similar letters	مِثْلَيْنِ
Ikhfaa	To hide	اِخْفَاءُ
Sagheer	Small	صَغِيْرُ

LESSON 7

Sifat	A description, quality or characteristic	صِفَةٌ
Laazimah	Necessary and always there	لَازِمَةٌ
'Aaridhah	Sometimes there and sometimes not – it was explained under mushtarak	عَارِضَةٌ
Mutadhaadda	Opposites; completely different to each other	مُتَضَادَّةٌ
Ghayr mutadhaadda	Not having an opposite	غَيْرُ مُتَضَادَّةٍ
Hams	A soft voice	هَمْسٌ
Jahr	A clear, open voice	جَهْرٌ
Shiddah	Strong and loud voice	شِدَّةٌ
Rikhwah	Weak and quiet voice	رِخْوَةٌ
Isti'laa	Full mouth and high	اِسْتِعْلَاءٌ
Istifaal	Empty mouth and low	اِسْتِفَالٌ
Itbaaq	To close and join	إِطْبَاقٌ
Infitaah	To open and separate	اِنْفِتَاحٌ
Izlaaq	Easy	إِذْلَاقٌ
Ismaat	Silent	إِصْمَاتٌ
Tawassut	In between *shiddah* and *rikhwah*; moderate; It is not a *sifat* on its own, but rather, in between *shiddah* and *rikhwah*	تَوَسُّطٌ

LESSON 8

Qalqalah	Echo	قَلْقَلَة
Safeer	Whistle	صَفِيْر
Leen	Soft	لِيْن
Tafash-shii	To spread	تَفَشِّيْ
Inhiraaf	On one side	اِنْحِرَاف
Takreer	To double or repeat	تَكْرِيْر
Istitaalah	To make long	اِسْتِطَالَة

LESSON 9

Madd	To stretch	مَدّ
Tuwl	To be long	طُوْل
Tawassut	Moderate or average	تَوَسُّط
Qasr	Short or clipped	قَصْر
Asli	Original and ever-present	أَصْلِيّ
Far'ee	Secondary	فَرْعِيّ
Muttasil	Inside a word	مُتَّصِل
Munfasil	Between 2 words; separated	مُنْفَصِل
Aaridhii	Temporary	عَارِضِيّ
Wajib	Needed or necessary	وَاجِب
Laazim	Compulsory; must be done	لَازِم

107

Muqatta'aat	Un-joined letters	مُقَطَّعَاتْ
Kalimi	Inside a word	كَلِمِيّ
Harfi	Inside a letter	حَرْفِيّ
Muthaqqal	Heavy	مُثَقَّلْ
Mukhaffaf	Light	مُخَفَّفْ

LESSON 10

Waqf	To stop	وَقْفْ
Iskaan	Pray with a *saakin*	إِسْكَانْ
rawm	To pray very short	رَوْمْ
Ishmaam	To make round; to make a circle with the lips is called *ishmaam*.	إِشْمَامْ
Saktah	To stop the sound – but not the breath	سَكْتَةْ

24385796915651994

6438791006437692

612